2

D1394901

A little course in...

Sewing

A little course in...

Sewing

DK

LONDON, NEW YORK, MUNICH, MELBOURNE, DELHI

Project Editor Becky Shackleton
Project Art Editor Gemma Fletcher
Senior Editor Alastair Laing
Managing Editor Penny Warren
Managing Art Editor Alison Donovan
Senior Jacket Creative Nicola Powling
Jacket Design Assistant Rosie Levine
Pre-production Producer Sarah Isle
Senior Producers Jen Lockwood, Seyhan Esen
Art Directors Peter Luff, Jane Bull
Publisher Mary Ling

DK India
Assistant Art Editors Karan Chaudhary, Tanya Mehrotra
Senior Art Editor Ivy Roy
Managing Editor Alka Thakur Hazarika
Deputy Managing Art Editor Priyabrata Roy Chowdhury

Written by Hilary Mandleberg,
Caroline Bingham, Becky Shackleton
Photographers Andy Crawford, Dave King

First published in Great Britain in 2013 by
Dorling Kindersley Limited, 80 Strand, London WC2R 0RL
Penguin Group (UK)

2 4 6 8 10 9 7 5 3 1
001–187848–Jan/2013

Copyright © 2013 Dorling Kindersley Limited

All rights reserved. No part of this publication may be
reproduced, stored in a retrieval system, or transmitted in any
form or by any means, electronic, mechanical, photocopying,
recording, or otherwise, without the prior written consent
of the copyright owners.

A CIP catalogue record for this book is available
from the British Library.

ISBN 978 1 4093 6519 8

Printed and bound by Leo Paper Products Ltd, China

Discover more at
www.dk.com

Contents

1 Start Simple

2 Build On It

3 Take It Further

Build Your Course

This book is divided into three sections: Start Simple, Build On It, and Take It Further. These chapters are carefully structured to help you learn new skills and techniques and then cement your increasing knowledge by completing the step-by-step projects.

Getting Started

The key to successful sewing is careful preparation and planning. The introduction to this book guides you through different fabrics and haberdashery items and shows you the equipment you'll need to complete your projects successfully, from needles and thread to scissors, irons, and sewing machines. It also gives helpful advice on choosing fabrics and using templates.

Templates

The simple templates given on pp.178–185 are essential to many of the projects within the book. Make sure you refer to pp.30–31 so that you know exactly how to use them.

Some templates are real size and will simply need to be traced

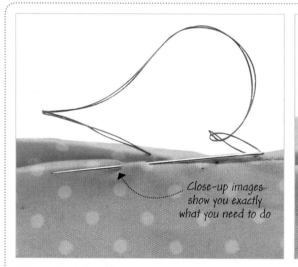

Close-up images show you exactly what you need to do

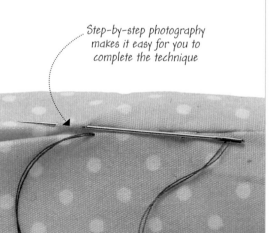

Step-by-step photography makes it easy for you to complete the technique

Key technique

The key techniques show you everything you need to know to complete your projects successfully and appear immediately before the projects they are needed for. They range from simple skills such as forming hand stitches and creating a double hem, to advanced techniques such as inserting a zip or sewing an elasticated waistband.

*Details about
each task are
pointed out*

1 In every project, illustrated step-by-step text guides you carefully through the process of cutting, pinning, and sewing. The text explains in detail exactly how to get the best possible results.

Careful! To guide you and give further useful advice, key information about each step is flagged up, preventing you making common mistakes.

The perfect **Project**

These handy boxes show you what your final project should look like and give you advice on how to achieve this while avoiding any common mistakes.

*The key features of
your item are
flagged up*

*Annotation tells
you what your
project should
look like*

The "Perfect Project" boxes appear at the end of each step-by-step project and explain the key features that your newly-made item should have, whether that be sharp corners, aligned Velcro™ strips, or strong handles.

Practical advice is given to help you achieve these things as well as to prevent any problems occuring. This box also contains any other relevant information relating to your project, such as adjusting the size or number of pockets.

Now turn over to find out more ▶ ▶ ▶

Essential **Equipment**

NEEDLES

Needles are a key part of your sewing kit. There is a wide range on the market to suit a variety of fabrics and projects but as you get started you will only need to work with a few different types. Keep your needles in a needle case: if they are together in a small container, they will become blunt and then you risk damaging your fabric as you sew.

Sharps
This is a general-purpose needle for hand sewing. Choose sizes 6 to 9 for most of your needs.

Crewel
This needle with its long, oval eye can be threaded with multiple strands. Choose it when using embroidery thread.

Milliner's or Straw
Traditionally used for making straw hats, this long, thin needle is for general hand sewing and tacking. Sizes 8 and 9 are the most popular.

Quilting or Betweens
These very short, fine needles are perfect for fine hand sewing, such as quilting, which demands quick, even stitching.

Darner's
This long, thick needle with a large eye is designed for use with wool or other thick yarns and for sewing multiple layers.

Wire needle threader
This handy gadget takes the pain out of threading a needle with a small eye. For instructions on how to use it, see p.34.

PINS

Although pins are the smallest of your sewing tools, they have important jobs to do, like holding a pattern in place while you cut the fabric out or securing a seam as you machine-stitch it. They come in a wide range of styles, lengths, and thicknesses, each designed for a different purpose. Beginners only really need household and dressmaker's pins but invest in more types as you progress.

Household
These general-purpose pins are of medium length and thickness. They are suitable for most types of sewing.

Dressmaker's
These pins are ideal for beginner sewers. They are similar to household pins but are slightly longer.

Pearl-headed
The heads on these pins make them easy to pick up and use. They are a little longer than household pins.

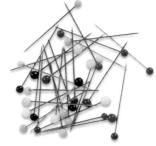

Glass-headed
These pins are a little shorter than pearl-headed pins. Their glass heads won't melt if you iron over them.

Flowerhead
The flat heads on these long pins can be ironed over and machine-stitching is easy with the pins in place.

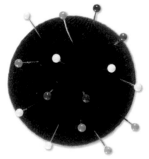

Pin cushion
Store your pins in a pin cushion to help keep them clean and sharp. See pp.64–69 to make your own.

SEWING THREADS

When you are starting on your sewing journey you might be a bit bewildered by the range of sewing threads on the market. Varying in thickness and fibre content, each type is designed for a specific purpose, so pick carefully – if you choose the wrong thread, you risk spoiling your project.

Cotton thread
Smooth and firm, 100% cotton thread should be your choice for sewing all cotton fabrics.

Polyester all-purpose thread
As its name suggests, this is suitable for all types of fabric. It is probably the most popular type of thread.

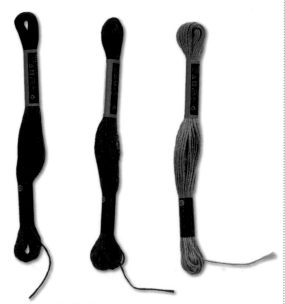

Overlocker thread
Specially designed for use with an overlocker machine (see p.20), this thread will break if you use it on your regular sewing machine.

Embroidery thread
This loosely twisted 6-strand, slightly glossy cotton thread is sold in small skeins. Use it for hand embroidery (see pp.56–59).

CUTTING TOOLS

Sewing inevitably involves some cutting. You may be cutting large pieces of fabric, trimming off the ends of thread, cutting into tiny corners, cutting through machine stitching you no longer need, or neatening the edges of fabric. Always buy the best quality cutting tools you can afford and the most comfortable; they will last you a lifetime.

Cutting shears
These are the scissors you will return to time and time again to cut large pieces of fabric. Choose a size that is comfortable to hold.

Trimming scissors
These handy little scissors are useful for trimming away surplus fabric and neatening the ends of machine stitching.

Paper scissors
Cutting through paper will dull the blades of your fabric scissors, so use these instead for cutting out paper templates or snipping around pattern pieces.

Pinking shears
These shears have blades that cut through the fabric in a zigzag pattern so the fabric won't fray. Use them to neaten seams (see p.78).

Embroidery scissors
These are small and very sharp. You will obviously use them for embroidery but they are also good for cutting into tight corners.

Seam ripper
This is your tool for removing machine stitching. Its little hook slides under the stitches and the sharp blade at the base cuts the thread (see p.175).

MEASURING TOOLS

Taking accurate measurements when you are sewing is one of the keys to success. You may have to measure the width of a seam or hem, the opening for a zip, or the length of a piece of ribbon or elastic. If you progress to dressmaking, you will also have to measure body dimensions to ensure a perfect fit.

Tape measure
This is your essential measuring tool. The one shown has metric and imperial measurements.

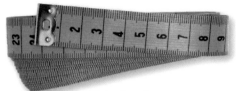

Extra-long tape
This is usually 300cm (10ft) long – twice the length of a normal tape measure. It will be useful if you progress to making soft furnishings.

Sewing gauge
Measuring only 15cm (6in), this handy tool with a sliding tab is useful for small measurements such as hems.

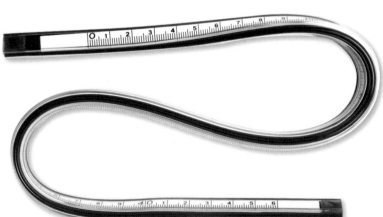

Flexible ruler
This bendy plastic ruler is perfect for measuring curved shapes.

Retractable tape
Keep one of these in your bag when you're shopping. You never know when you'll need to measure something.

MARKING TOOLS

When you need to position something very precisely – a pocket or a hemline, for example – you may find it useful to mark your fabric in a more lasting way than by using pins. When choosing your marking tool, always test it out first to make sure that the marks don't become permanent.

Tailor's chalk
Tailor's chalk readily brushes off fabric and comes in a variety of colours.

Chalk propelling pencil
Choose from a variety of coloured leads to insert in this pencil. The leads can be sharpened.

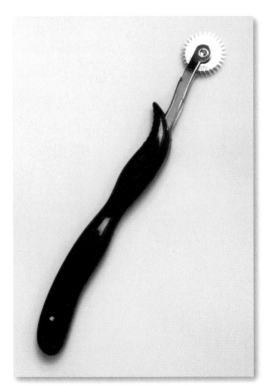

Water- or air-soluble pen
Use this pen to make marks that can be removed either with a spray of water or by leaving to air-dry. Be sure not to press over the marks or they will become permanent.

Chalk pencil
Use to draw accurate lines then remove with the little brush on the end.

Tracing wheel and carbon paper
When you progress to using bought paper patterns, these tools will be invaluable for transferring pattern markings to your fabric. Test first though as you may not able to remove the marks from all fabrics.

HABERDASHERY ITEMS

Haberdashery is the collective term used to describe all the varied bits and pieces that you will need for your sewing projects. The term includes buttons, different types of fasteners such as hooks and eyes, snap fasteners, and Velcro™, plus trimmings, ribbons, zips, and elastic.

BUTTONS

The sky's the limit when it comes to buttons. They can be made from a multitude of materials and can be any shape. Some are attached through holes on the surface while others have a shank on the back that you stitch through onto the fabric.

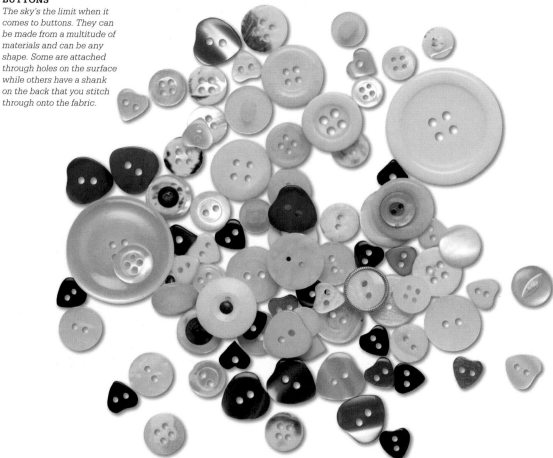

SIMPLE FASTENERS

Hooks and eyes (right, above) and snap fasteners (right, below) come in different sizes, shapes, and colours. Some are decorative and are meant to be on show. Velcro™ (far right) is great as a fastener for children's clothing or projects such as an eReader case (see pp.84–89).

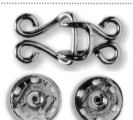

**HOOKS AND EYES AND
SNAP FASTENERS**

VELCRO™

TRIMMINGS

There's a world of fabulous trimmings out there to use as great finishing touches. You could trim a child's skirt with ric-rac braid, add a bobble trim to a tote bag or decorate a pocket with a row of coloured lace or braid.

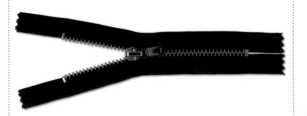

RIBBONS

Ranging from very narrow to very wide and made from a wide variety of yarns, ribbons can be plain or patterned. Some feature metallic threads or wired edges.

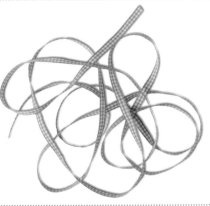

ZIPS

Choose the correct zip for your project – from lightweight nylon zips through cotton zips with brass teeth to open-ended jacket zips and concealed zips.

ELASTIC

Elastic is available in widths and types to suit all sorts of sewing projects. It even comes in colours other than white and you can buy special decorative elastic too.

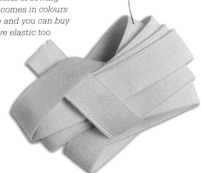

SEWING MACHINE

Once you move on to using a sewing machine, you'll be amazed at how quickly you can sew. Most machines now use computer technology, which makes it easy to set the type of stitch, its length and, where appropriate, its width. Many machines also embroider. Make sure you put in plenty of practice on your sewing machine before you embark on a complete project.

Speed Control
This slide controls the
speed at which you sew

Thread Take-Up Lever
The thread passes through on
its way from the spool to the
eye of the needle

Tension Dial
Use this to control the
stitch tension on the
upper thread

Buttonhole Sensor
This pull-down sensor
automatically judges the size of
buttonhole to suit your button

Buttons
Use for reverse,
locking, and moving the
needle up and down

Presser Foot
This holds the fabric in place.
Different feet are used for
different processes (see p.19)

Needle Plate
This plate is marked with
guides to help stitch seams
of various widths

**Detachable
Extension Table**
Remove this to leave you
with a narrow "free arm"
– useful for sewing sleeves
and trouser legs

JANOME

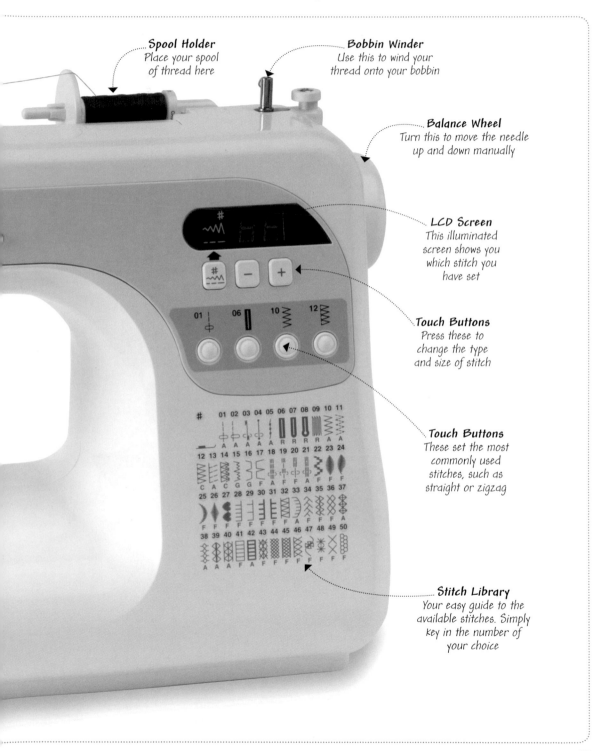

Spool Holder
Place your spool
of thread here

Bobbin Winder
Use this to wind your
thread onto your bobbin

Balance Wheel
Turn this to move the needle
up and down manually

LCD Screen
This illuminated
screen shows you
which stitch you
have set

Touch Buttons
Press these to
change the type
and size of stitch

Touch Buttons
These set the most
commonly used
stitches, such as
straight or zigzag

Stitch Library
Your easy guide to the
available stitches. Simply
key in the number of
your choice

SEWING MACHINE ACCESSORIES

Your machine will come with a number of accessories such as a set of needles, some bobbins – these hold the machine's lower thread – and some presser feet. Three types of presser foot are shown here but there are many more to choose from, depending on your requirements.

Plastic bobbin
Some machines require a plastic bobbin. Check your machine instructions before buying as using the wrong bobbin can affect the tension of the stitch.

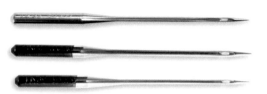

Machine needles
Different needles are designed to cope with different fabrics. A size 60 needle is for the lightest-weight fabrics while a size 120 is for the heaviest.

Metal bobbin
This is one of several types of metal bobbin that are on the market. Always use the same type as came with your machine.

PRESSING AIDS

If you press your work well and correctly at each stage, you will end up with a really neat, professional finish. Your basic kit is shown here. If you progress to more advanced sewing, or even tailoring, you will need to invest in some more specialized equipment.

Iron
Choose a fairly heavy, good-quality steam iron with a shot-of-steam option. If your iron is too light, you'll have to press down harder for a good result.

Pressing mitten
This padded glove – rather like an oven glove – gives you more control over the area you are pressing.

Blind hem foot
Use this foot with a blind hem stitch to work a blind hem (see p.93).

Overedge foot
This foot holds your fabric in place while you sew an overedge stitch, which is used to neaten a raw edge (see p.78).

Zip foot
Attach this to either the right or the left side of the needle so you can stitch close to the teeth of a zip.

Ironing board
Buy the longest ironing board you can, especially if you plan to make a table cloth or apron, and make sure it is height-adjustable.

Pressing cloth
Use a fine, see-through cloth made from a natural fibre between your iron and the fabric to prevent marks and scorching.

Overlocker

Once you are confident in using your sewing machine, you may want to invest in this handy piece of equipment. It provides a professional, no-fray edge to your fabric and speeds up your work by removing the surplus edge of the fabric as you sew. An overlocker can also be used to make gathers, while more advanced models offer various other options, such as making pintucks or sewing elastic. You can buy a machine for use with three to eight threads. This one has four threads.

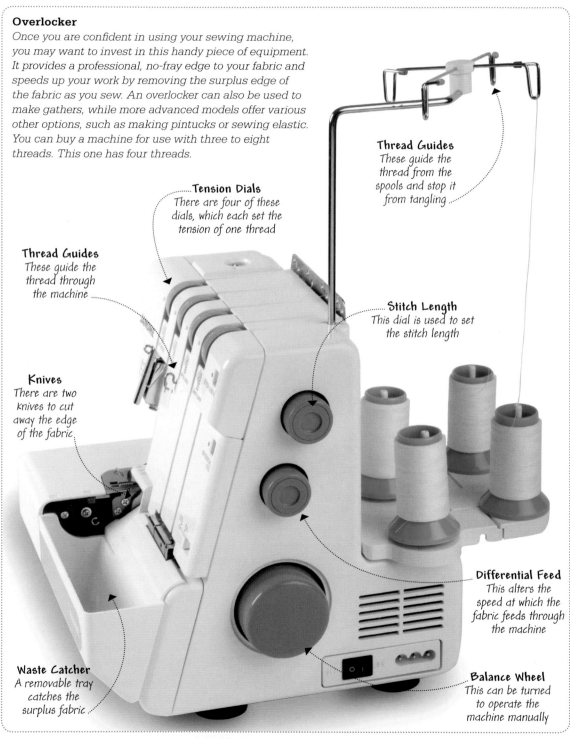

Thread Guides
These guide the thread from the spools and stop it from tangling

Tension Dials
There are four of these dials, which each set the tension of one thread

Thread Guides
These guide the thread through the machine

Stitch Length
This dial is used to set the stitch length

Knives
There are two knives to cut away the edge of the fabric

Differential Feed
This alters the speed at which the fabric feeds through the machine

Waste Catcher
A removable tray catches the surplus fabric

Balance Wheel
This can be turned to operate the machine manually

Overlocker stitches

Your overlocker will make stitches that are similar to a sewing machine's zigzag stitches (see p.78), but the result looks more professional. If you have an overlocker that works with four threads, you can use it to form 2-thread, 3-thread or 4-thread overlock stitches. 3-thread and 4-thread are the most commonly used.

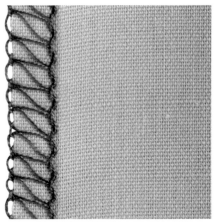

3-thread overlock stitch
This stitch is ideal for knits or for seams that are not under a lot of strain. It can also be used decoratively.

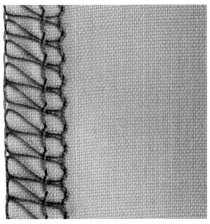

4-thread overlock stitch
This stitch is extra-secure as it has a safety stitch running down the middle of the overlock.

Overlocker foot
This is the standard presser foot that you will use for most projects.

Overlocker needles
These are specialized ballpoint needles. They make a large loop in the thread that is caught by the machine's loopers to create the stitch.

Gathering foot
Use this together with the differential feed (see opposite) to create lovely, even gathers.

Understanding **Fabrics**

Weft, warp, and grain

All woven fabrics have warp threads running the length of the fabric from left to right and weft threads passing under and over the warp threads, running from top to bottom. Warp threads are stronger and so are less likely to stretch than weft threads. The "grain" is the direction in which the warp and weft threads lie – there is a warp grain and a weft grain. The selvedge is the tightly woven, non-fraying edge that runs parallel to the warp grain.

Aligning patterns
If you are cutting out a patterned fabric, ensure that you cut the straight edge in alignment with, or at a right angle to, the selvedge to ensure that the fabric doesn't look wonky once it's been sewn.

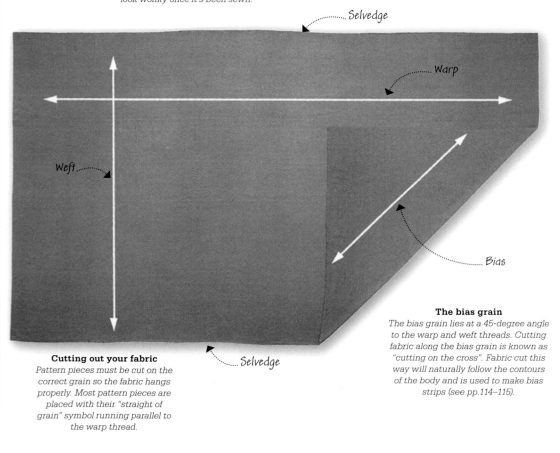

Selvedge

Warp

Weft

Bias

Selvedge

Cutting out your fabric
Pattern pieces must be cut on the correct grain so the fabric hangs properly. Most pattern pieces are placed with their "straight of grain" symbol running parallel to the warp thread.

The bias grain
The bias grain lies at a 45-degree angle to the warp and weft threads. Cutting fabric along the bias grain is known as "cutting on the cross". Fabric cut this way will naturally follow the contours of the body and is used to make bias strips (see pp.114–115).

Fabric Construction

There are three main types of fabric construction – woven, knitted, and non-woven – all of which have been used for centuries. You must use the correct type for your project and adapt your sewing technique accordingly. Knits, for example, are best sewn using a ballpoint needle and either an overlocker or a zigzag stitch.

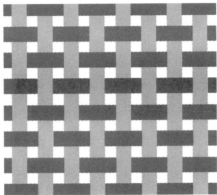

Plain weave
The weft thread passes under one warp thread and over another in this, the simplest type of woven fabric.

Warp knit
Knitted fabrics consist of interlocking looped yarns. In warp knits, the yarn zigzags the length of the fabric. Weft knits are more like hand-knitting, with one thread running horizontally through the fabric.

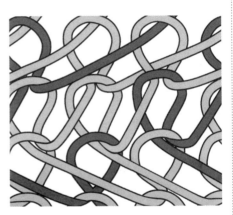

Non-woven fabric
This is constructed from long fibres that have been bonded together. Wet wipes and teabags are examples, but in sewing, the most common non-woven you will come across is felt (see p.27).

Your Fabric Choices

Choosing the right fabric for your project is key but for a beginner sewer especially, it can be hard to know where to start. Pattern manufacturers and sewing and craft magazines always give details of recommended fabrics; follow their suggestions and you won't go wrong. Cotton is a natural fibre and in general, cotton fabrics are easiest to sew. They won't slip as you work and they can easily be pressed with a steam iron. On top of that, they launder well.

Calico
This rather stiff cotton fabric is usually unbleached, which gives it a homespun look. It is inexpensive and strong and is available in many weights, from fine to very heavy. Dressmakers use calico to make a toile – a test garment that shows whether a pattern will fit correctly. You can also use it to make sturdy bags and aprons (see pp.150–156).

Chambray
Also known as cambric, this fine cotton has a coloured warp thread and a white weft thread, which give it a subtle two-tone effect, rather like denim (see opposite). Available in its original blue colour, you can also find it in soft pink, green, and grey, as well as with checks and stripes. Chambray feels soft and smooth and wears well. It's a great choice for blouses, dresses, and childrenswear, and for making projects such as lavender hearts (see pp.40–44) and bunting (see pp.116–120).

Gingham

This traditional two-coloured checked cotton fabric is made up of groups of white and coloured warp and weft threads. The effect is of criss-crossing lines with a darker colour where the coloured warp and weft threads interweave. The size of the checks can vary. Gingham looks pretty used for skirts and dresses, or in projects such as drawstring bags (pp.48–53) or a phone case (see p.90), but you need to line up the pieces carefully.

Denim

Denim has a diagonal, or twill, weave, with a coloured warp thread and a white weft thread, like chambray (see opposite). This traditional, tough workwear fabric comes mainly in blue, but also in other colours. It is now often woven with elastic for the fashion market to give it some stretch. If you want a traditional finish, you will need to topstitch using a contrast thread.

Jersey

Originally made of wool, you can now find cotton and synthetic jersey, too. Whatever fibres it is made from, it is a knitted fabric, with more or less stretch, depending on its specific construction. It is very comfortable to wear, which is why it is the choice for teeshirts and much sleepwear. It also drapes well, so is often used for women's dresses and blouses. When sewing, use a stretch stitch with a ballpoint needle and, if possible, an overlocker to neaten the seams.

Muslin

This fine, loosely woven cotton fabric is usually available in white or in its unbleached form. Air moves freely through it, so muslin clothing and muslin curtains are a good choice for hot climates. Use muslin as an interlining and as a pressing cloth (see p.19) and use it in the kitchen for straining jams and marmalades. You will fill a muslin pouch with dried lavender when making lavender hearts (see pp.40–44).

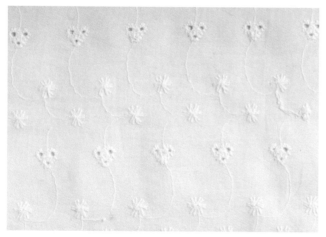

Broderie Anglaise

This fine cotton or poly-cotton mix usually comes in white or pale pastel colours. It has self-coloured embroidery and the patterns incorporate small holes edged with stitching. You can buy fabric with all-over broderie anglaise or with a broderie anglaise border, in which case you will have to plan carefully how you cut your pattern to ensure the border is at the hem edge. Broderie anglaise is pretty for trimming pockets, bags, and children's clothes.

Linen

Coarser than cotton, linen is another natural fibre. Its main disdavantage is its tendency to crease, but creased linen is now something of a fashion statement. Linen comes in all weights from very fine to heavy suiting. Like cotton, linen takes dye well so you can buy it in an enormous range of colours. Linen yarn is often uneven, which produces a fabric with a slubbed effect, as here. Use it to create attractive tote bags (see pp.106–111) or lavender hearts (see pp.40–44).

Cotton and Linen mix
Because it is expensive, linen can sometimes be woven together with cotton, as here. The cotton and linen may have been mixed together in the yarn or the fabric may have mixed warp and wefts threads. This cotton/linen fabric has a textured weave that makes it a good choice for sturdy tote bags (see pp.106–111) and aprons (pp.150–157).

Felt
Most felt is made from wool by the wet felting method. Friction and water together make the microscopic scales on the wool fibres bond together. This means that felt is a non-woven fabric and will not fray when cut. You can buy felt in a huge array of bright, even glittery, colours. Available in different thicknesses, felt is sold by length or in small squares for craft use.

Wadding
Use wadding wherever you need to add some thickness to your sewing project, for example to stuff a fabric shape to make it three-dimensional, such as a pincushion (see pp.64–69), or for protection, like the wadding used in an eReader case (see pp.84–89). Wadding comes in different weights and thicknesses and can be made from natural fibres such as cotton, wool, silk, or even bamboo, from synthetics such as polyester, or from a mixture.

Buying and Using Fabric

Modern life gives us so much choice that it can sometimes be hard to know where to begin. Here is some advice on how to buy, cut, and make the most of your fabric, as well as some fabric-buying tips to help you narrow down your options.

Where to buy

Fabrics are sold in the fabric sections of department stores, in specialized fabric shops, and online. So which is best? You'll have more choice if you go online and you may end up paying less; online shopping may also be best if you don't live near a good department store or fabric shop. But if you're a beginner sewer, it really does pay to see and feel the fabric before you buy. It's also a good way to familiarize yourself with the huge array of fabrics that are out there.

What to buy

Most fabrics come in wide rolls that are mainly 150cm (60in) and 115cm (45in) wide. Your pattern instructions will advise you on the correct width and length to buy. Beginners should steer clear of slippery and stretchy fabrics and heavy fabrics like corduroy. Instead, stick to cottons and cotton mixes. These are easier to sew and generally cheaper, so if you make a mistake – and everyone does sometimes! – it won't be an expensive one.

Prepare to cut

Always cut out on a smooth, flat surface like a dining table. Cutting out on the floor is inconvenient and a definite no-no if the floor is carpeted. Your pattern pieces won't lie flat and your cuts won't be accurate.

For professional-looking results, lightly press your paper pattern pieces with a dry iron before you use them, to ensure that they lie flat. Wash, dry, and iron washable fabrics, and iron dry-clean only fabrics. Once ironed, your fabric will lie perfectly flat as you cut and washable fabrics will do any shrinking before you've put in all the work instead of after.

Finally, lay your pattern pieces out on the fabric, following the suggested cutting layout in your pattern or project instructions. Position all the pieces before you start to cut to make sure that everything's going to fit on the fabric, and that all the pieces align with the pattern on the fabric, then pin in place. Before you make that first cut, check you haven't dropped a pattern piece on the floor, then off you go!

P.S.

After you've cut your fabric and completed your project, don't throw away any decent-sized leftovers. You never know when you might need a scrap to patch a hole or to use as an embellishment for another sewing project. And if nothing else, you can always start to make a patchwork quilt (see p.134).

Fabric-buying tips

Before you commit to buying a fabric, ask yourself the following questions:

• Is this fabric one of the types recommended for my pattern or project?

• Does this fabric suit the project that I'm going to make?

• Will this fabric hang correctly for my project? Unroll a little to check.

• Do I like the way the fabric feels? Is it too stiff, too soft, or too scratchy?

• Does the fabric fray easily?

• Does the fabric shed fibres easily?

• Does the fabric stretch enough or too much?

• Is the fabric washable? If it's hand-wash or dry-clean only, will that be a problem for upkeep in the future?

• Is the fabric wide enough for my pattern?

• Have I allowed enough extra material so that the pattern will match across all the pieces of my template?

Using a Template

SCALING UP YOUR TEMPLATE

On pp.178–185, you will find the templates you'll need for the projects in this book. For most projects the template is the actual size and you will just need to trace it, but the templates on pp.184–185 will need to be enlarged. The simplest way to do this is to use the dimensions given and recreate the shape for yourself on tracing paper, making sure that all of your dimensions match those given.

Sometimes you may want to make something to a different size from the size stated in the book. For example, you may want to make a heart-shaped cushion from the lavender heart template. Assuming your template is 5cm (2in) tall and you want your finished item to be 25cm (10in) tall, divide the finished size by the size of the template and multiply by 100. This gives you the percentage by which you need to enlarge the

template, i.e. 25cm (10in) divided by 5cm (2.5in) equals 5. Multiply this by 100 to get 500. You need to enlarge your template by 500 per cent. Place the relevant page directly onto a photocopier and set the copier to enlarge to this amount.

If you ever have to enlarge a template to a size that is too big for a standard sheet of A3 or A4 paper, you will need to do it in two or more stages. First make "registration marks" (small circles or a dotted line) at several points around the edge of the template. Assuming you only need two stages – sufficient for most projects – enlarge one half of the template at a time, making sure that the registration marks appear on both of the photocopies. Finally, align the registration marks, tape the two photocopied halves together – and voilà, you have your scaled-up template.

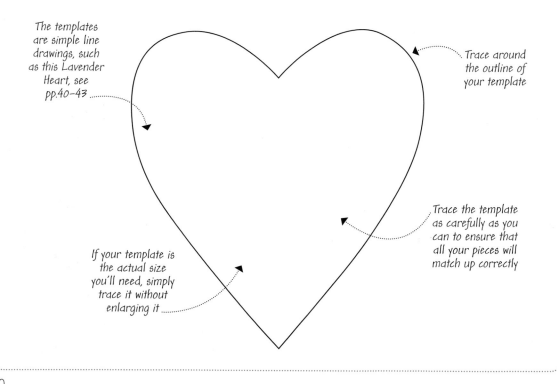

The templates are simple line drawings, such as this Lavender Heart, see pp.40–43

Trace around the outline of your template

Trace the template as carefully as you can to ensure that all your pieces will match up correctly

If your template is the actual size you'll need, simply trace it without enlarging it

MAKING A TEMPLATE INTO A PATTERN PIECE

Once you have scaled-up your template to the required size, you are ready to turn it into a pattern piece that guides you when cutting your fabric. Pattern pieces are generally made of tracing paper; the fabric is visible through the tracing paper, which makes it easier to position the pattern correctly.

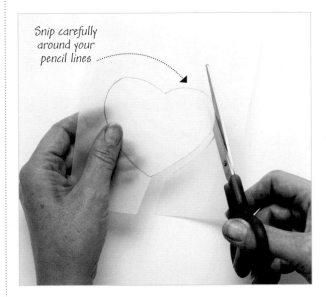

Snip carefully around your pencil lines

Tracing and Cutting

Place a piece of tracing paper over the scaled-up template and trace the outline of the image using a soft pencil. Cut out the shape with a sharp pair of scissors. If you are using a template that does not need scaling-up, simply trace directly from the template.

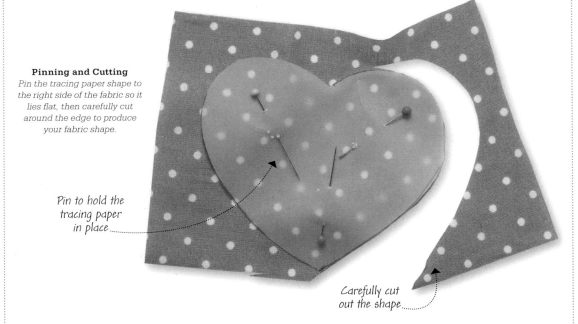

Pinning and Cutting

Pin the tracing paper shape to the right side of the fabric so it lies flat, then carefully cut around the edge to produce your fabric shape.

Pin to hold the tracing paper in place

Carefully cut out the shape

1

Start Simple

Sewing is enjoying a bit of a comeback and not just because people want to save money. It's about injecting individuality into the everyday items we use. Here you'll master the very basics of sewing, from threading a needle through simple hand-stitching to sewing on a button and tackling simple embroidery stitches. Using these techniques, you'll learn to make a lavender-stuffed heart, a drawstring bag, pretty felt flower brooches, and a pin cushion in next to no time.

In this section learn to make:

Lavender Hearts
pp.40–44

Drawstring Bags
pp.48–53

Felt Flower Brooches
pp.60–63

Pin Cushions
pp.64–69

How to **Thread a Needle**

Thread can have a mind of its own, either fraying madly or refusing to go through the eye of the needle at all. Use a needle with a large eye and cut the end of the thread with sharp scissors to make things easier. If your thread is too long, it can get tangled as you sew, so make sure it's no longer than the distance between your elbow and your fingertips.

1

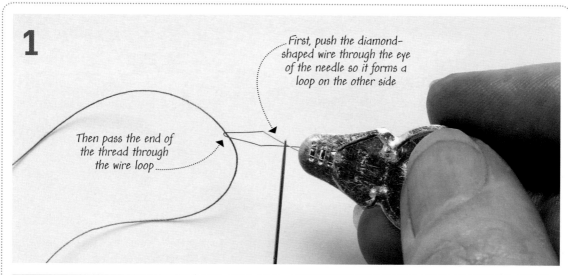

First, push the diamond-shaped wire through the eye of the needle so it forms a loop on the other side

Then pass the end of the thread through the wire loop

2

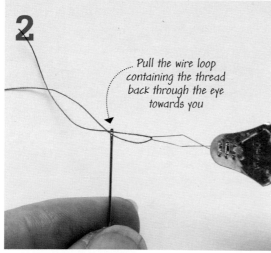

Pull the wire loop containing the thread back through the eye towards you

3

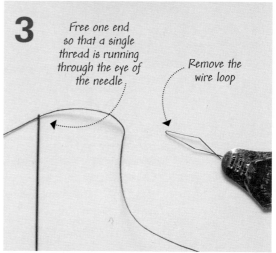

Free one end so that a single thread is running through the eye of the needle

Remove the wire loop

Using a needle threader

A needle threader consists of a diamond-shaped piece of very fine, very flexible wire attached to a little handle. The threader is especially useful for threading a needle that has a small eye. Hold the threader carefully by its handle as you guide it towards the needle.

Threading by hand

1

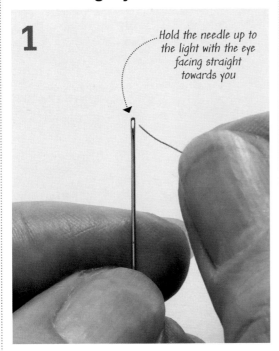

..Hold the needle up to the light with the eye facing straight towards you

2

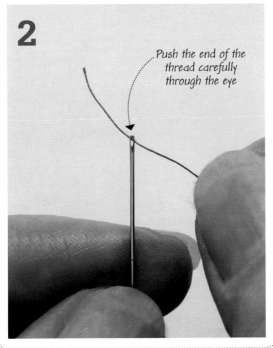

.Push the end of the thread carefully through the eye

Tip If the thread starts to fray, either recut the end or moisten it with dampened fingers.

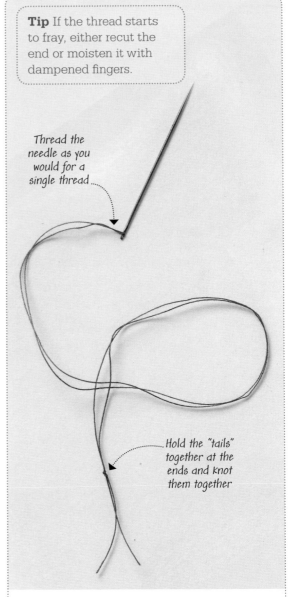

Thread the needle as you would for a single thread ..

..Hold the "tails" together at the ends and knot them together

Tying double thread

If you need a stronger thread, perhaps for sewing on buttons, hooks and eyes, or snap fasteners, use a double thread. Pull the thread through the eye of the needle until you have two "tails" of the same length, then knot the two ends together.

How to **Sew Simple Hand Stitches**

Even in the age of the modern sewing machine, hand sewing techniques are still often used to prepare fabrics for permanent stitching. Remember, there's no point stitching anything without firmly securing the thread at the end. If you don't, sooner or later your thread will come out and you'll be left with a hole where your seam used be.

Running stitch

You'll use this easy stitch time and time again for a range of uses, from joining two pieces of fabric to embroidery stitches. If you use a matching thread the stitches will be hard to spot, but you can use a visible running stitch in a contrasting colour for decoration if you prefer. Bring your needle through the fabric from the back to the front. Working from right to left, pass the needle through the fabric to behind, then bring it out again, making a stitch. Repeat.

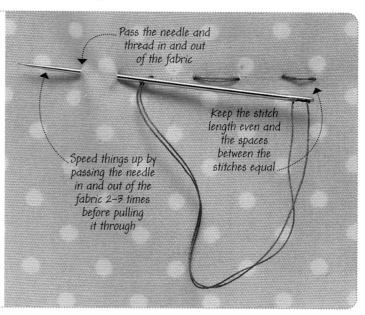

Pass the needle and thread in and out of the fabric

Keep the stitch length even and the spaces between the stitches equal

Speed things up by passing the needle in and out of the fabric 2–3 times before pulling it through

Use a simple running stitch

You don't need to keep the stitch length even, but the stitches should not be too long

Tip End your row of tacking stitches with a backstitch (see opposite) rather than a knot to make it easier to remove the tacking stitches later.

Tacking stitch

You'll need this temporary stitch to hold two pieces of fabric together until you have completed the permanent stitching. It's also sometimes known as a basting stitch. Use a contrasting colour thread with a knot tied in the end. With the right sides of the fabric together, working from right to left, bring your needle through the fabric to the upper side. Continue with long running stitches, although be sure not to make them too long or they won't hold the pieces of fabric together.

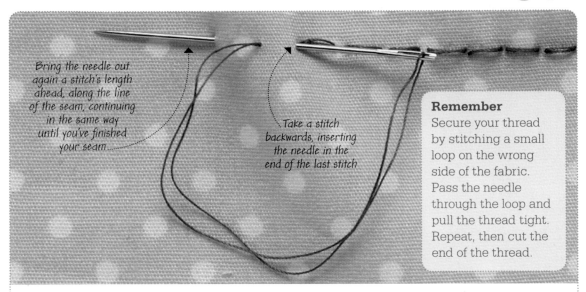

Bring the needle out again a stitch's length ahead, along the line of the seam, continuing in the same way until you've finished your seam......

Take a stitch backwards, inserting the needle in the end of the last stitch

Remember
Secure your thread by stitching a small loop on the wrong side of the fabric. Pass the needle through the loop and pull the thread tight. Repeat, then cut the end of the thread.

Backstitch

Backstitch looks like machine stitching on the right side. It is one of the strongest hand stitches, so it's useful wherever you need a strong seam. Start with right sides of the fabric together. Working right to left, bring your needle through the fabric to the upper side.

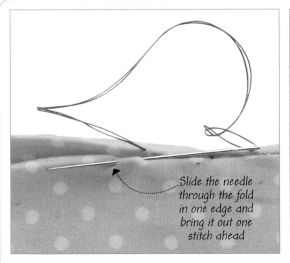

Slide the needle through the fold in one edge and bring it out one stitch ahead

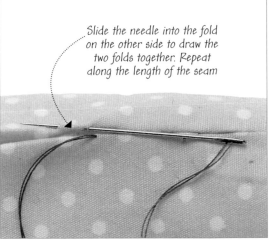

Slide the needle into the fold on the other side to draw the two folds together. Repeat along the length of the seam

Slip stitch

This is an almost invisible stitch that is used to join two folded edges together, such as the opening in a cushion. You can also use it to attach a folded edge to an unfolded piece of fabric. To do this simply pick up one or two threads of the unfolded fabric on your needle as you make your second stitch back through the folded fabric edge.

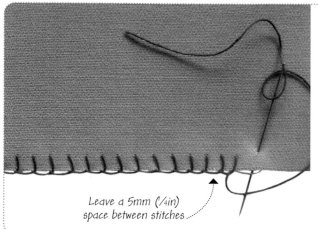

Leave a 5mm (¼in) space between stitches

Blanket stitch

This stitch is useful for neatening edges and for decoration. Working from left to right, point the needle towards you and insert it through the right side of the fabric, roughly 5mm (¼in) from the edge. As the needle appears at the edge, wrap the thread underneath it, then pull the needle through. Repeat for all subsequent stitches. Remember to secure the thread at the start with a small backstitch (see p.37).

Herringbone stitch

This stitch holds two pieces of fabric together, but allows for some movement. It's often used for securing the hem of a skirt made from a stretchy fabric, such as a knit. Working from left to right, take your needle through to the front of the unfolded fabric. With the thread above the needle, take a small stitch from right to left through the folded fabric, near the edge of the fold. Then, do the same above the fold so that the thread crosses itself. Repeat.

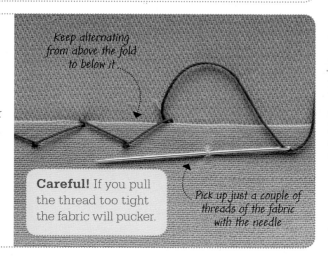

Keep alternating from above the fold to below it

Careful! If you pull the thread too tight the fabric will pucker.

Pick up just a couple of threads of the fabric with the needle

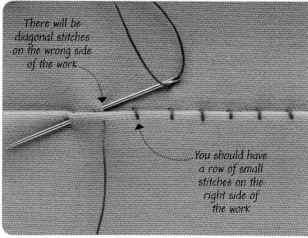

There will be diagonal stitches on the wrong side of the work

You should have a row of small stitches on the right side of the work

Fell stitch

This strong stitch is worked from the right side of the fabric and is used to join a folded edge to a flat piece of fabric. You can use it to attach linings and to finish attaching bias binding. Take the needle through to the right side of the fabric just below the fold. Then make a small stitch perpendicular to the fold into the unfolded fabric. Next take the needle diagonally left into the work and bring it out again just below the fold.

How to **Sew on a Button**

Buttons have been used as fasteners for about two thousand years. In the early days they were made from seashells, but nowadays they are made from a huge range of materials, both natural and synthetic, including bone, shell, nylon, plastic, and metal.

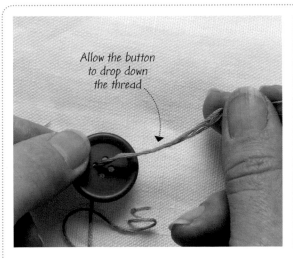

Allow the button to drop down the thread

1 Knot the thread and sew from the back of the fabric to the front. Put the needle through one of the holes in the button.

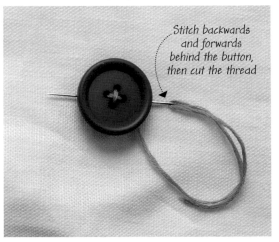

Leave a small amount of thread at the back of the button

2 Push the needle through the opposite hole in the button and through to the back of the fabric. Don't pull the thread tight.

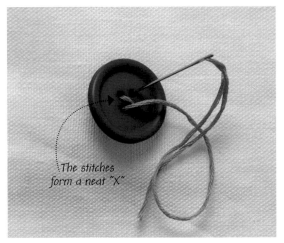

The stitches form a neat "X"

3 Continue stitching up and down through the button and the fabric. With this four-hole button, the stitches form a cross.

Stitch backwards and forwards behind the button, then cut the thread

4 Make a stitch from the back of the fabric to the front, but take the needle out under the button instead of pulling it through.

Make a Lavender Heart

Lavender has been used for centuries to perfume clothing
and ward off moths. This simple hand-sewn project brings
the old-fashioned lavender bag bang up to date.
Once you've made it, chances are you won't want
to hide it away in a drawer or cupboard.

You will need:
Three templates from p.181, Lavender Hearts A, B, and C • Pencil • Three fabrics: two cotton,
one felt • Fabric scissors • Pins • Pinking shears • Embroidery silk • Needle • Circle of muslin
10cm (4in) in diameter • Dried lavender • Wadding • Rustic twine or ribbon

1 Trace the templates onto a piece of paper using a pencil and cut out the heart pattern pieces. Fold the main fabric in half, wrong sides together, and pin template A to it. Cut around the template with pinking shears – by cutting the front and back out together you ensure that they are exactly the same size and shape. Use templates B and C to cut out two small heart appliqués – one from felt, one from cotton.

Cut close to the edge to make the most of your fabric

Pin the pattern securely so it can't move as you cut around it

Use a bright thread colour to make a feature of your stitches

2 Using three strands of embroidery silk, stitch the appliqué shapes onto the piece that will form the front of your heart, placing as shown. Use a simple running stitch.

Tip Don't feel limited to using running stitch – why not try out some of the other embroidery stitches given on pp.56–59.

3 Pin the front and back pieces together securely and using three strands of embroidery silk, stitch around the outside edge using a small running stitch. Start and end on a straight edge. Leave a 6-cm (2½-in) gap and enough thread to finish the seam later on.

Remember Secure your thread at the start of your line of stitches, otherwise the front and back pieces will start to come apart.

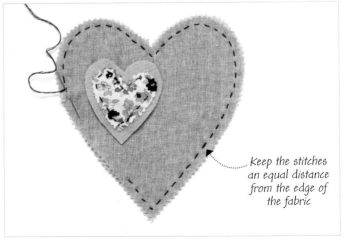

Keep the stitches an equal distance from the edge of the fabric

4 Sew around the outer edge of the circle of muslin using a running stitch. Leave the needle attached. Place a pinch of lavender in the centre of the muslin and then pull the thread to gather the edges inwards, enclosing the lavender. Sew the pouch closed. Securing the lavender in this way keeps it in place and prevents it showing through the outer fabric.

... Add the lavender once you are ready to tighten the thread

Allow the fabric to concertina slightly as you sew ...

The lavender ball needs to sit in the centre of the heart ...

Push wadding right into the point of the heart ...

5 Using wadding, begin to stuff the heart through the gap you left in the stitching. Once the heart is about half full, insert the lavender muslin ball. Continue to fill, pushing wadding around the ball so that it is firmly held in the centre of the heart. Make sure the heart is plump and evenly stuffed.

6 Once you are happy that you have inserted enough wadding, pin up the gap and stitch it closed, continuing the line of running stitch. Secure the thread firmly at the end of your stitches so that the front and back of the heart cannot come apart. If the heart feels lumpy, manipulate it with your fingers to get an even shape.

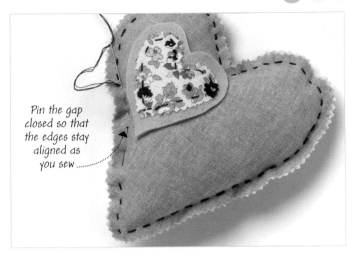

Pin the gap closed so that the edges stay aligned as you sew ......

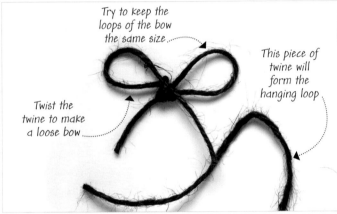

Try to keep the loops of the bow the same size .....

This piece of twine will form the hanging loop

Twist the twine to make a loose bow .....

7 There are many materials you could use to hang your hearts, such as rustic-looking twine, ribbon, or embroidery silk. To create a hanging loop from rustic twine, twist a length into a loose bow. Work out how long you want your hanging loop to be, cut another piece of twine to this length, and feed both ends through the centre of the bow. Stitch through the centre of the bow to secure the loop in place and then trim off the ends of the loop. Sew the bow onto the top corner of your heart – stitch it so that it sits on top of the line of stitches around the edge.

Insert the loop into the bow and stitch the two pieces of twine together

Trim off the excess twine once the hanging loop is secure

43

The perfect **Lavender Heart**

You can't really go far wrong with these simple hearts. Wonky shapes and uneven stitching can add to their rustic charm, but here are a few things to keep in mind.

Stitch the bow on top of your existing line of stitches

The heart should be plump

The stitches should be evenly sized and spaced

Even padding

The heart should be plump and evenly filled with wadding. If the stuffing feels a little uneven once you have sewn up your heart, you should be able to manipulate it using your fingers to get a smooth shape – be careful when you do this though, as you want the lavender bag to sit in the centre of the heart, cushioned with wadding on all sides. If you feel that your heart doesn't have enough padding in it, you may want to carefully unpick the stitches and insert some more.

Symmetrical shape

The shape should be symmetrical, with even stitching around the outside edge. If you cut your fabric slightly wrong, or your stitches weren't spaced evenly from the edge, your heart might look a little wonky. Don't worry though, as slight imperfections give this project charm. If you're really unhappy, try again, keeping the pieces of fabric tightly pinned together to make it easy to sew in a straight line.

Calming scent

The lavender scent makes these hearts perfect for hanging in a wardrobe or popping under your pillow. Over time, the scent will fade. You could remove the muslin bag and replace the lavender. Alternatively, simply keep the old heart for decoration and make new, freshly scented versions.

Also learn to make ▶ ▶ ▶

Make **Alternative shapes**

Once you have mastered the technique for making lavender hearts, why not adapt the heart shape and embellish it in different ways, or make other decorative shapes? You could make a smaller heart, using template B (see p.181), or you could lengthen the point of the heart and add a little curve to it (below right). Alternatively, you could make a completely different shape, such as the bird (right), which uses the templates on pp.180 and 183. Its contrasting felt wing and ribbon legs make an attractive decoration to hang around the house.

CUTTING YOUR PATTERN

You can use almost any simple outline you like as long as you make sure that the front and back pieces are exactly the same shape and size. The best way to do this is to cut one paper pattern and pin it to your fabric, which should be folded in half, right sides inwards. Use pinking shears to give a zigzag edge, or use fabric scissors for a straight edge.

CREATING YOUR SHAPE

Before sewing the front and back together, add any decoration you want, such as the bird's wing and eye, or any other embellishments. Secure these neatly using embroidery thread. Using the same techniques as for the lavender heart, stitch your front and back pieces together leaving a 6-cm (2½-in) gap along one edge. If you are making a bird and wish to attach ribbon legs, pin these into position before you sew – place them so that 1cm (½in) of the ribbon sits inside the bird – this will secure them. Stuff the shape with wadding and then neatly sew up the hole.

Tip A hanging loop of ribbon secured with a button in a contrasting colour can look very attractive. Choose a contrasting ribbon, make it into a hanging loop, cross the ends over, and pin them in position at the top of the heart. Make sure that when the button is on top, the ends of the ribbon poke out a little way beyond the edge of the button. Stitch the button in place where the ends of the ribbon cross and through the stitching round the edge of the heart. Trim the ends of the ribbon so they are of equal length.

Lavender Bird

Lavender Hearts

Uses for your lavender shapes

These simple shapes can look stunning if you use a few of them to form a decorative wall hanging or even a mobile for a child's cot. Choose attractive ribbons and twine, and experiment with different shapes. Stuff them with wadding but leave out the lavender if you are giving them to children.

Make a mobile by hanging the shapes from an attractive wooden or wire coat hanger using soft-coloured ribbons. Suspend the shapes so that they hang at different lengths. Don't use buttons or other small decorations, which could come loose and become a choking hazard.

Create your own Christmas tree decorations in simple shapes such as stars or Christmas trees – ensure that you push your stuffing well into the triangular corners of these shapes. Consider giving them a festive fragrance using cinnamon sticks (see right), cloves, or winter berry-scented oil.

For an attractive wall hanging, take a long piece of rustic twine or ribbon and attach a heart to each end. Hang this from a hook above your bed, or from a wardrobe or cupboard door. Alternatively, make three hearts – one large and two small – and attach them along a piece of ribbon with the largest in the middle as the centrepiece.

Attach your keys to one of these padded shapes and you'll be less likely to lose them. Ensure that your hanging loop is securely attached to the padded shape before sliding it onto your key chain. Use a sturdy ribbon or twine.

Alternative fillings

If you don't like the scent of lavender, or you fancy experimenting with something different, why not replace it with another fragrance? Don't feel limited to using dried, ground herbs – a few drops of scented oil or a couple of cinnamon sticks can be just as effective.

Cinnamon is one of the quintessential Christmas scents and makes a great alternative to lavender. On a protected surface, lay your cinnamon sticks down flat and drill a small hole through the middle. Slide them onto your hanging loops. These shapes make perfect seasonal decorations or gifts.

Dried herbs such as peppermint make a wonderful, fresh alternative to lavender. Grind the leaves up in a pestle and mortar and then secure them in a muslin bag, as for lavender.

Oils are available in a wide range of fragrances. Apply a few drops of oil to a square of muslin and then bunch this up. When you insert it, ensure that this square of muslin is surrounded with wadding, as if the oil comes into contact with the main fabric it will leave a stain.

Pot pourri should be used in the same way as dried lavender. There are a lot of different fragrances to pick from – simply choose your favourite and fill a muslin bag with it.

Cinnamon sticks

Peppermint

Scented oils

Pot pourri

Make a Drawstring Bag

Fed up with characterless plastic storage boxes?
Make this simple drawstring bag in a printed cotton
of your choice for a more personalized way to store
small toiletry items or a collection of hair accessories.

You will need:
Fabric: 15 x 22cm (6 x 9in) • Fabric scissors • Pins • Needle • Thread
Ribbon: 30cm (12in) long • Safety pin

1 Fold your oblong of fabric in half along the long edge, right side to right side. With the fold to your left, pin the doubled fabric together along the bottom edge and up the right-hand edge, stopping 2.5cm (1in) from the top – this will allow you to create the channel for the drawstring in Step 3. Place the pins facing outwards – this will make them easy to remove as you sew – and space them 2.5cm (1in) apart. Make sure all the edges are neatly aligned.

Tip If your fabric is striped or patterned, cut so that patterns run parallel to the edges of the bag.

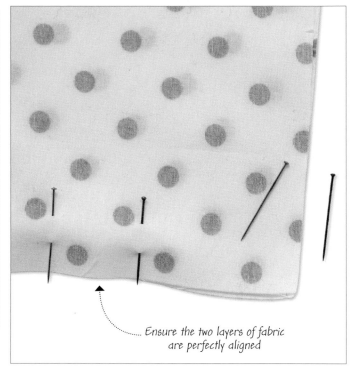

Ensure the two layers of fabric are perfectly aligned

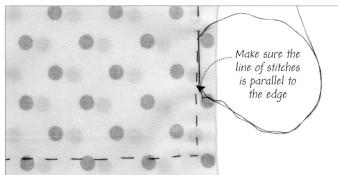

Make sure the line of stitches is parallel to the edge

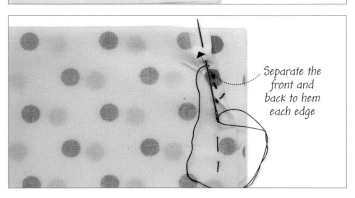

Separate the front and back to hem each edge

2 Starting in the bottom left-hand corner, secure the thread and sew along the bottom edge and up the right-hand side, stopping at the pins. Use a short, even hand running stitch about 1cm (½in) from the edge. Remove each pin as you reach it. Your bag now has a front and a back. At the top of the seam, in the unstitched area, fold the edge of the fabric over to make a narrow hem and sew in place. Repeat for both the front and the back.

3 Fold the top 2cm (¾in) of the fabric over to make a hem, and pin securely into place. You will thread your ribbon through this channel, so ensure that the ribbon is narrow enough to fit.

Careful! Once you have pinned the fabric in place, doublecheck that the turnover is an even depth all the way round.

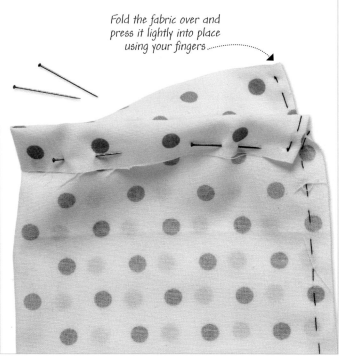

Fold the fabric over and press it lightly into place using your fingers

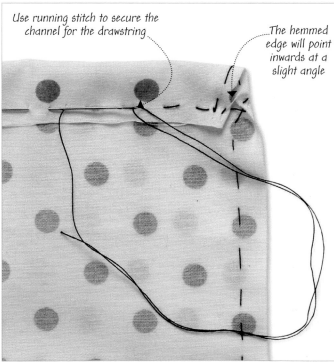

Use running stitch to secure the channel for the drawstring

...The hemmed edge will point inwards at a slight angle

4 Begining on the front right hand side, use short, even hand running stitches to secure the folded fabric in place. Remove the pins as you go. Secure the end of the thread once you reach the end of the turnover.

Remember Keep your stitches as neat and even as possible, as they will be visible once the bag is turned the correct way out.

A safety pin makes threading the drawstring easy

5 Attach a safety pin to one end of your piece of ribbon and slide it into the channel. Work the safety pin along with your fingers until it comes out at the other end. Knot the ribbon at the length you want and then turn the bag inside out so that it is ready to use.

Tip To work out how long you want your drawstring to be, pull the bag closed before you knot the end – you will see how much excess ribbon you are left with.

The perfect **Drawstring Bag**

Careful, neat hand stitching is the key to ensuring your drawstring bag holds its shape well and looks good. Choose a ribbon in a contrasting pattern for a quirky look.

Securely knotted ribbon

Drawstring ribbon

Tidy, even stitching

Neat, square corners

Neat shape

The bag should have a straight rectangular shape and sharp corners. Be careful when sewing to make sure that you stitch a straight line parallel to the edge of the fabric, and that you create a right angle of stitches in the bottom corner, otherwise when you turn the bag inside out, the shape will not be rectangular. Also bear in mind that your drawstring bag cannot hold a great amount of weight and that if you stitch too close to the edge you risk creating weak points in the seam.

Secure ribbon

The drawstring ribbon adds a lovely decorative touch, and enables you to hang your bag wherever you like. If you have used a very silky ribbon, you may have trouble getting the knot to hold at the end of the drawstring. Using a matching thread, put a few stitches into the knot to hold it in place. Alternatively, re-thread the bag using a ribbon with a slightly rougher texture.

Also learn to make ▶ ▶ ▶

Alternative Drawstring Bag

There is more than one way to make these useful little bags, so try this alternative method, which uses two ribbons and two pieces of fabric rather than one. This type of bag is ideal as a gift bag.

MAKING YOUR BAG

Cut two pieces of fabric, each 15 x 11cm (6 x 4½in) and two pieces of ribbon, 30cm (12in) long. Place the fabric pieces on top of each other, right sides together, and pin them. Sew up the bottom and two sides, starting and finishing 2.5cm (1in) from the top of each side in order to make the channels for the drawstring ribbons. As in Step 2, on p.49, separate the two layers. Fold the four 2.5-cm (1-in) unstitched tops of fabric over to make narrow hems and sew them in place using running stitch. Fold the top 2cm (¾in) of each side of the bag over to make the channels, iron these down, pin securely, and then sew into place with hand running stitch.

Thread the ribbons through – thread the first ribbon through the left hand side of the front piece, out through the right hand side, then back into the right hand side of the back piece and out through the left. Knot the ends together. Repeat with the other ribbon from the other side so that when the two knotted ends are pulled, the bag closes. Turn the bag inside out and it is ready to use.

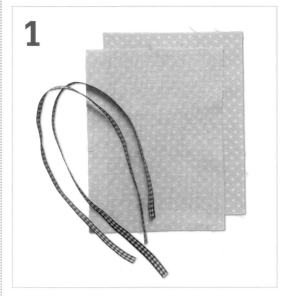

1

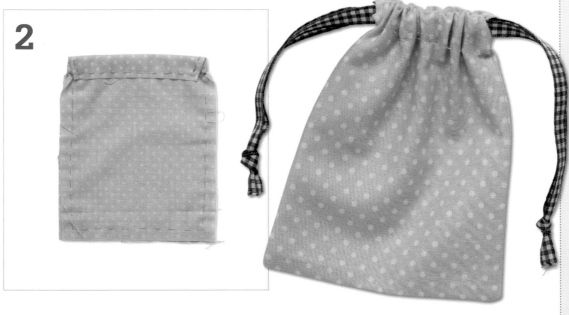

2

How to **Make Puffs**

These decorative circular rosettes, or puffs, can be used to add a finishing touch to many of your craft projects, including bags, bunting, and purses. They are very simple to make in any size, although bear in mind that the puff will end up about half the size of the circle you cut out initially.

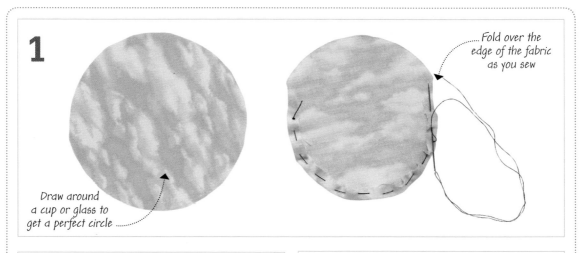

1

Draw around a cup or glass to get a perfect circle

Fold over the edge of the fabric as you sew

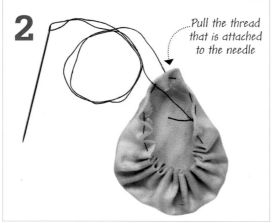

2

Pull the thread that is attached to the needle

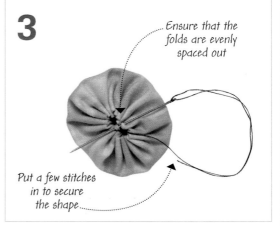

3

Ensure that the folds are evenly spaced out

Put a few stitches in to secure the shape

Cut a circle of fabric to your desired size. Thread a needle and tie a knot in the end then, folding the edge of the circle to the wrong side by about 7mm (¼in) as you go, secure the folded edge with a neat, even running stitch. Do not stitch too close to the fold. When you have sewn all the way round

back to your starting point, gently pull on the thread. The folded edge will bunch up and be drawn into the centre of the circle. Once you have drawn the circle in tight, secure the puff by stitching the edges together at the centre. Do not stitch through to the front of the puff.

Using Puffs

There are many ways in which you can use your puffs – decoratively, just as they are, adorned with buttons or ribbons, or stitched together like patchwork pieces to make a throw or decorative wall hanging.

Use puffs as wheels on any of your crafty projects that feature trains and cars, such as the bunting featured on p.121. Not only are the puffs the perfect shape for the wheels but they also add a decorative touch, which is far more interesting to look at or touch than a simple circle of fabric.

Tip Make the puffs in different sizes, textures, and colours to add some variety to your design.

The circular shape lends itself to a flower motif. Attach the puff to craft projects, such as the tote bag featured on p.113. Make a feature of the flower by sewing a button into the centre and adding a line of embroidery stitches beneath it for the stem and leaves.

Tip Experiment with the different embroidery stitches shown on pp.56–59 to embellish your flower – create twisting stems, curling vines, or grass for the flower to sprout from.

Transform the puff into a brooch by stitching a fastening or safety pin onto the back. Cut a circle of fabric about 15cm (6in) in diameter and sew your puff as shown opposite. Select a button to form the centrepiece of your brooch and cut six lengths of ribbon about 10cm (4in) long. Cut the ribbon at a 45-degree angle with a pair of sharp fabric scissors to prevent it from fraying. Sew the button onto the middle of the puff, with the six strands of ribbon securely fastened underneath it. Alternatively, fold each ribbon piece in half to make a loop and put a stitch in the ends to secure. Attach the ribbon loops in place underneath the button.

Tip Use a stiff cotton to form the puff so your brooch will hold its shape well.

Bunting (see p.121)

Tote bag (see p.113)

How to **Sew Embroidery Stitches**

Now it's time to move on and learn how to do some simple
embroidery stitches. Master these and you'll be able to use
them to decorate the felt flower brooches on pp.60–63, as well
as in various other projects. But first, you'll need to invest in
some embroidery thread and a crewel needle (see p.8 and p.10).

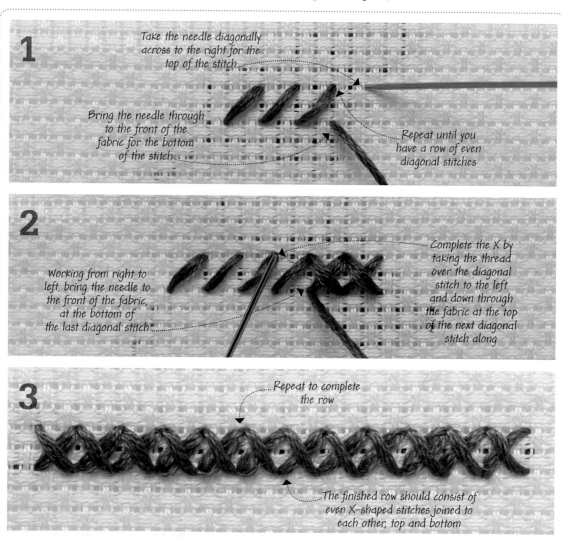

1 Take the needle diagonally across to the right for the top of the stitch.

Bring the needle through to the front of the fabric for the bottom of the stitch.

Repeat until you have a row of even diagonal stitches

2 Working from right to left, bring the needle to the front of the fabric, at the bottom of the last diagonal stitch.

Complete the X by taking the thread over the diagonal stitch to the left and down through the fabric at the top of the next diagonal stitch along

3 Repeat to complete the row

The finished row should consist of even X-shaped stitches joined to each other, top and bottom

Cross stitch

This simple X-shaped stitch has been used
for centuries all over the world. You may have
seen it decorating household linens. Work the
cross stitches on their own or next to each
other to form a row, as shown here. Always
start by working from left to right.

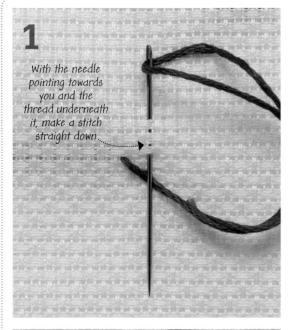

1 With the needle pointing towards you and the thread underneath it, make a stitch straight down.

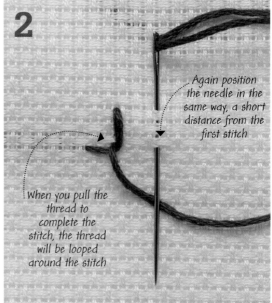

2 Again position the needle in the same way, a short distance from the first stitch

When you pull the thread to complete the stitch, the thread will be looped around the stitch

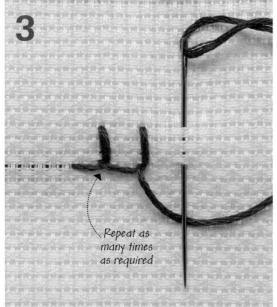

3 Repeat as many times as required

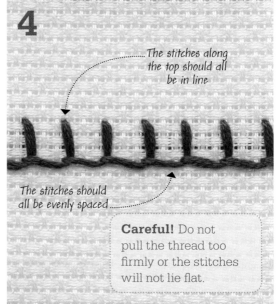

4 The stitches along the top should all be in line

The stitches should all be evenly spaced

Careful! Do not pull the thread too firmly or the stitches will not lie flat.

Blanket stitch

You can use blanket stitch for finishing any sort of an edge or simply for decoration. It can also be used for appliqué – attaching a fabric shape to another piece of fabric. Work from left to right. Start by bringing the needle from the back of the fabric to the front.

57

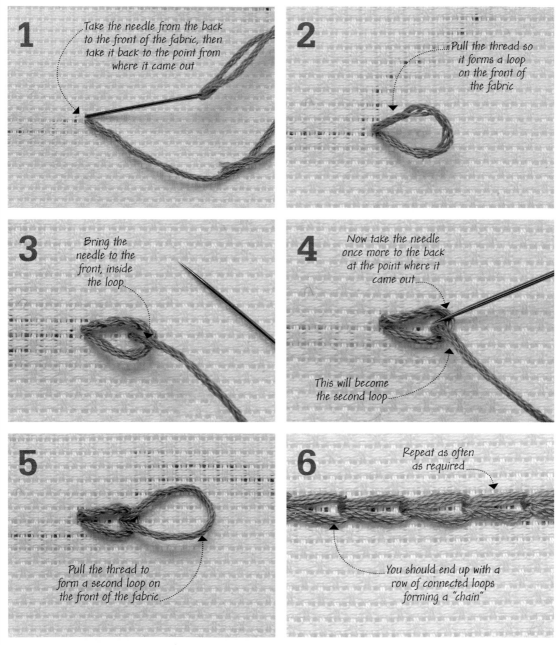

1 Take the needle from the back to the front of the fabric, then take it back to the point from where it came out

2 Pull the thread so it forms a loop on the front of the fabric

3 Bring the needle to the front, inside the loop

4 Now take the needle once more to the back at the point where it came out. This will become the second loop

5 Pull the thread to form a second loop on the front of the fabric

6 Repeat as often as required. You should end up with a row of connected loops forming a "chain"

Chain stitch

When worked in a continuous row, as shown above, chain stitch creates a chain-like effect. Alternatively, after Step 3, take your needle over the loop and through to the back of the fabric. This will hold the loop in place and produce a stitch that looks like a leaf or petal.

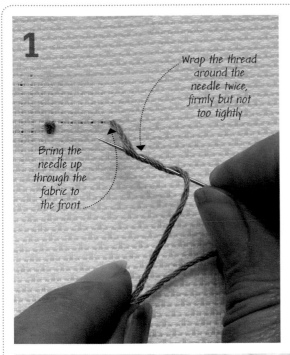

1 Bring the needle up through the fabric to the front

Wrap the thread around the needle twice, firmly but not too tightly

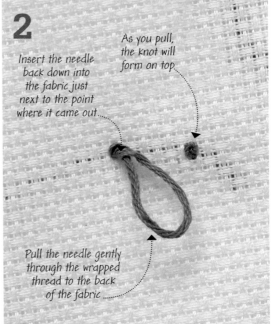

2 Insert the needle back down into the fabric just next to the point where it came out

As you pull, the knot will form on top

Pull the needle gently through the wrapped thread to the back of the fabric

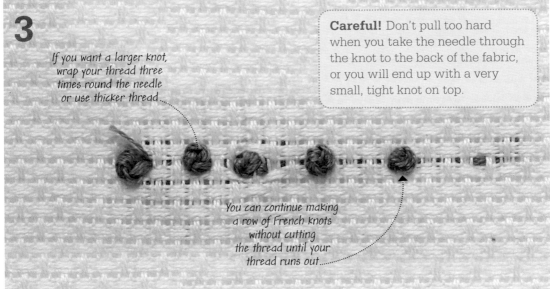

3 If you want a larger knot, wrap your thread three times round the needle or use thicker thread

Careful! Don't pull too hard when you take the needle through the knot to the back of the fabric, or you will end up with a very small, tight knot on top.

You can continue making a row of French knots without cutting the thread until your thread runs out

French knot

This classic stitch adds a welcome element of texture to your work. You can use these little knots for lots of decorative effects, either on their own or in groups. A single knot can be a flower centre, an eye, or a nose, while a group of knots works well as a flower head.

Make Felt Flower Brooches

If you buy these in the shops you can spend a small fortune, but felt flower brooches are deceptively easy to make. Use individually or in a group to add some pizazz to a beret, a jacket, a cardigan – or anything you care to pin them to.

You will need:

Templates from pp.178–181 • Fabric: felt in assorted colours; contrasting fabric to cover buttons and make leaves • Fabric scissors • Embroidery thread • Needle • Pins • Buttons Pinking shears • Brooch fastenings • Fabric or PVA glue

Daisies

1 Cut an oblong of felt 13cm (5in) long and 5cm (2in) wide. Fold the felt in half lengthways and crease it using your fingers. Secure the top edge with a few stitches and leave the needle in place. Hold the fabric with the crease towards you, and snip upwards along the entire length. Do not snip right through.

Secure the fabric using a needle and thread

Create a firm crease down the middle

Snip 2cm (¾in) cuts to form the petals

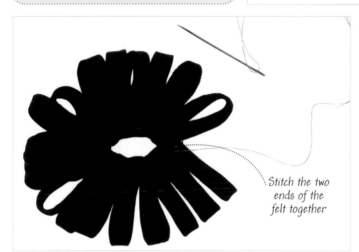

Stitch the two ends of the felt together

2 Using the needle and thread, sew along the long uncut edge of the felt with a running stitch. Once you reach the other end, pull the thread tight so that the felt gathers up into a tight circle. Sew the two ends together to form your ring of petals.

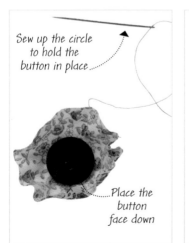

Sew up the circle to hold the button in place

Place the button face down

Sew through the button's holes to hold it in place

3 Cut a circle of fabric about twice the diameter of your button. Sew up the circle using the same technique as for a Puff, see p.54. Using a thread that will camouflage well with your fabric, sew the button to the backing fabric and secure it well.

Careful! Felt can be quite a stiff fabric, so take care not to prick your fingers when passing your needle through it.

4 If you want to add leaves to your flower, use pinking shears to cut out two teardrop shapes using the Leaf A and B templates on p.180. Using a matching thread colour, sew your brooch fastening to a square of felt, attaching it at both ends and in the middle, to make sure it is firmly held in place. Glue or sew the square of felt to the back of your flower to finish.

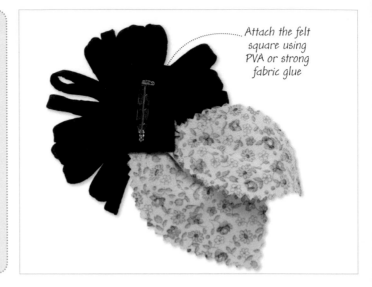

Attach the felt square using PVA or strong fabric glue

Layered petals

1 To create a layered flower, choose a a button for the centre and a selection of fabrics, including two colours of felt. Trace the patterns from p.178 and p.179 and cut out your flower shapes. Use pinking shears to cut out two circles for the flower centre.

Tip Felt is ideal for the petals as it won't bend or sag once in place.

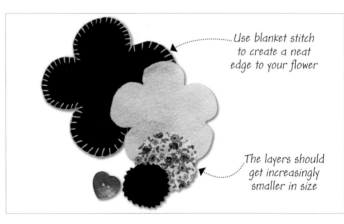

Use blanket stitch to create a neat edge to your flower

The layers should get increasingly smaller in size

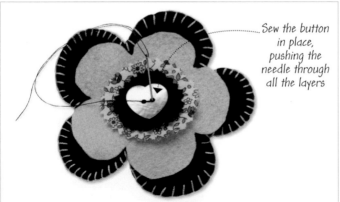

Sew the button in place, pushing the needle through all the layers

2 Lay out the shapes on top of each other, in decreasing size order. End with the button in the centre. Hold the layers in place as you sew through the holes in the button to secure them.

Tip Finish the flower off with a brooch fastening or attach it to a bag or hairband as decoration.

Roses

1 Trace the template for the felt rose (p.180) and cut it out. Pin it onto your felt and cut around it.

Tip Don't feel you have to play safe with rose-red felt. Why not experiment with any other coloured scraps of felt you have in your sewing basket?

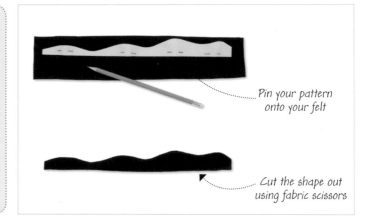

Pin your pattern onto your felt

Cut the shape out using fabric scissors

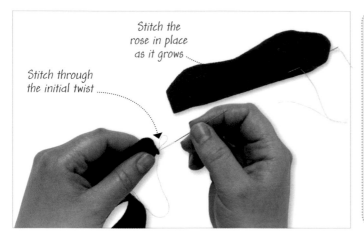

Stitch the rose in place as it grows

Stitch through the initial twist

2 Beginning at the narrower end, start to roll up the felt. Secure the initial twist at the bottom with a couple of stitches. Continue to roll, twisting the felt to form the rose shape, and securing at the bottom of the rose regularly with little stitches.

3 Using the templates on p.180, cut out some felt leaves using pinking shears. Embroider leaf markings using a running stitch (see p.36). Stitch the leaves onto the back of your roses and attach a brooch fastening onto the back.

Tip For a multi-coloured rose, snip the template in half and cut each half from a different colour felt. Stitch the pieces together to form one strip then roll up as in Step 2.

Embroider the leaves in a contrasting colour

Try using two colours in one rose

Make a Ladybird Pin Cushion

No insects were harmed during the making of this cute
ladybird pin cushion! Whether you're a beginner sewer
or a pro, a pin cushion helps you keep your pins to hand.
Our ladybird version will bring a smile to your face
every time you reach for a pin.

You will need:
Templates from p.182 • Fabric: black felt and polka dot cotton • Fabric scissors • Needle
Pins • White pearl-headed pins • Wadding

1 Trace the templates for the top and bottom of the pin cushion, the ladybird's head, the six legs, and the wing crease. Cut out your fabric pieces: use black felt for the body, head, six legs, and the wing crease. Use polka dot fabric to form the wings.

Tip When using the polka dot fabric for the ladybird's wings, position your template carefully before you pin it to get an equal number of spots on each wing.

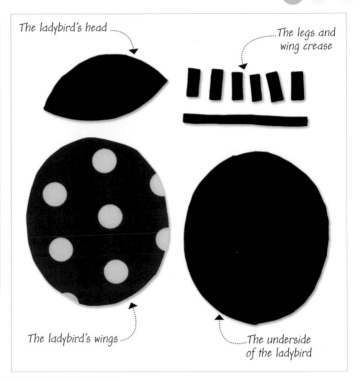

The ladybird's head

The legs and wing crease

The ladybird's wings

The underside of the ladybird

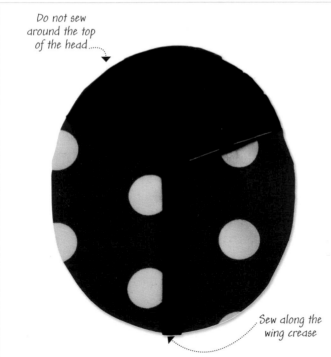

Do not sew around the top of the head

Sew along the wing crease

2 Position the ladybird's head and the wing crease on top of the polka dot body and pin them in place. Hand sew around the lower edge of the head and down the central wing crease to attach them to the polka dot body. Use a running stitch and a black thread, so that your stitches are camouflaged.

Remember You don't need to sew around the top edge of the head as this will be sewn in place when you join the top and bottom layers.

3 Arrange the six ladybird legs on either side of the polka dot body, facing inwards, towards the centre of the ladybird's back. When you turn the pin cushion inside out in Step 5, they will face outwards. Space them evenly.

Tip Position the legs closer to the ladybird's head than to its bottom. You will square it all up in Step 6 when you finish sewing the ladybird up.

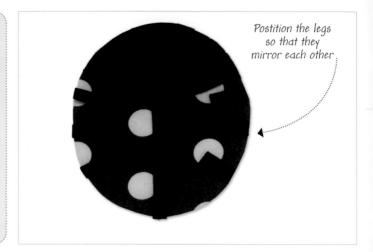

Postition the legs so that they mirror each other

4 Very carefully, place the underside of the ladybird on top, sandwiching the legs between the top and bottom. Take care not to move the legs as you pin through all the layers. Carefully turn the whole thing over and use a running stitch to hand sew round the entire ladybird, 1cm (½in) from the edge. Leave an 8-cm (3-in) gap in your stitching at the bottom of the body.

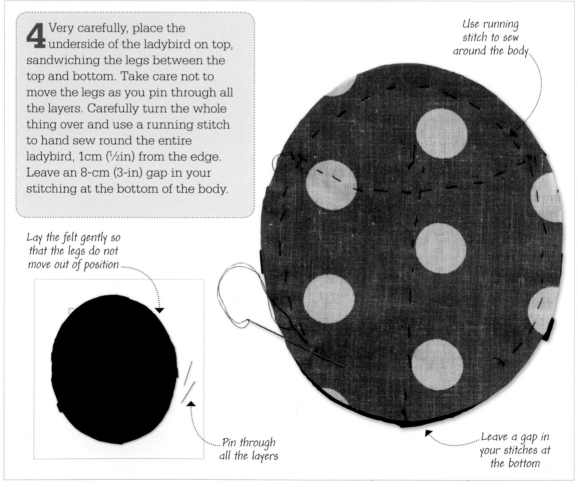

Use running stitch to sew around the body

Lay the felt gently so that the legs do not move out of position

Pin through all the layers

Leave a gap in your stitches at the bottom

5 Remove all the pins and carefully turn the ladybird inside out through the gap that you left in your stitches. Push your fingers right inside the body and along the seam, to make sure the fabric is stretched right out and that the shape is as round as possible. Stuff the ladybird with wadding through the gap in the bottom of the body.

Tip Fill your pin cushion with stuffing until it is plump and rounded. Manipulate the stuffing from the outside if you need to, to make sure that the shape is even.

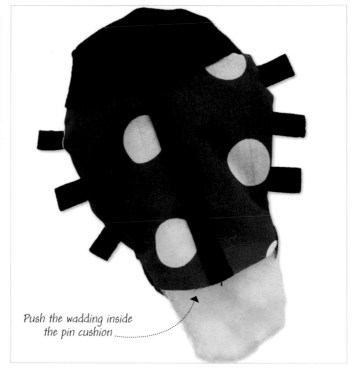

Push the wadding inside the pin cushion ....

..... Red thread will be hardest to spot against the polka dot fabric

...Hide all the untidy or raw edges by tucking them inside the pin cushion

6 When the pin cushion is full of stuffing and the fabric is taut, turn in the raw edges at the bottom of the body and pin them together. Use red thread and slip stitch to sew up the gap (see p.37).

Tip Use two white pearl-headed pins to make the eyes for your ladybird. Alternatively, use white embroidery silk and work two French knot stitches (see p.59).

The perfect **Ladybird Pin Cushion**

This must-have sewing accessory is very simple to create – just make sure that it is well-filled with wadding and that the legs are securely attached.

Well-rounded, firm shape

Legs should be evenly spaced

White pearl-headed pins in position for the eyes

Even, rounded shape

Your pin cushion should feel rounded and full of wadding, with no lumps or bumps. Not only will a plump ladybird look good, but the fabric will be nice and taut, making it easy for you to insert and remove pins. You will be able to manipulate any uneven areas once the gap in the stitching is sewn up, but if your pin cushion feels a little flat, consider unpicking the stitches and inserting a bit more wadding.

Well-spaced legs

The legs should be evenly spaced along the edge of the body. If they move around between Steps 3 and 4, some may end up longer than others or unevenly spaced. You won't know until you have turned the body through to the right side, by which time it will be too late. Just chalk it up to experience and ensure that the next time you make this project you pin everything more securely before stitching.

Also learn to make ▶ ▶ ▶

Alternative Shapes

This cheerful sunflower pin cushion will brighten up any desk or workspace and is very simple to make. You can stand it upright in a terracotta pot, or use it without its stalk and keep it in your sewing box.

PREPARING

Begin by cutting out your template pieces (see pp.182–183). Use pinking shears to cut out one inner circle of fabric and straight-bladed scissors for the two outer circles and the petals. Try to keep your petals as similar in size and shape as possible, but don't worry if they are slightly irregular – this will add to the charm!

SEWING

Using hand running stitch, sew the inner circle to the front of one of the outer circles to form the centre of the sunflower.

Arrange all the petals except two adjacent ones evenly around the edge of the second outer circle (this is the back of the sunflower), on the wrong side of the fabric. Ensure that each petal overlaps the edge by about 2cm (¾in) so that they are firmly anchored in place when you sew the front of the sunflower to the back. Carefully lay the front of the sunflower with its contrasting centre right side up on top of the wrong side of the back. Pin the front to the back all the way round, except in the area of the missing petals. You should have a gap of about 8cm (3in). This is where you will insert the wadding. If any petals feel loose, unpin them, slide them a little further in, and pin again.

Using hand running stitch, sew around the edge of the sunflower through all the layers, 1cm (½in) from the edge. Remove the pins as you go. When you reach the last pin, secure the thread. Fill the sunflower head through the gap with wadding until the fabric is taut. Pin your last two petals in place in the gap, ensuring that all the wadding is trapped inside the flower.

Sew up the gap using running stitch. If you want to add a stalk (see above, right) leave a gap of 1cm (½in) in your stitches.

Leave these two petals until last

CREATING A STALK

Cut a piece of bamboo cane about 20cm (8in) long. Cut a piece of green felt to the same length and about 4–5cm (1½–2in) wide. Lay the cane on top of the felt and fold in half lengthways so that the cane is completely enclosed. Sew the edges of the felt together around the cane using running stitch. The felt tube should be a snug fit. Insert the "stalk" through the gap in the edge of the flower. Add a few more stitches to hold the stalk securely. Fill your pot with a block of floristry foam and insert the sunflower in it. Alternatively, providing your pot doesn't have any holes, fill it with plaster of Paris, insert the sunflower, and leave to set.

Bug Bags and Simple Cushions

these small polystyrene balls online, from specialist craft and haberdashery suppliers, or from department stores.

Tip Be careful not to over-fill your bug bean bags or there is a risk that when you throw them around, they will burst on impact and scatter their contents everywhere.

LADYBIRD CUSHIONS

You can make a ladybird cushion any size you like simply by scaling up the templates for the ladybird pin cushion (see p.182). Follow the instructions as for the pin cushion (see pp.65–68). The cushions are sure to get grubby over time, so choose durable fabrics that you can spot-clean. You don't want to be opening the cushions up every few months to remove the stuffing and wash the covers.

ALTERNATIVE CUSHIONS

You don't have to stick to ladybird cushions. Almost any simple shape will work well, from circles to squares to rectangles. Just decide on the shape and size you want, make a template, cut your fabric (making sure of course that your front and back pieces are both exactly the same size and shape), and off you go!

Using exactly the same techniques as you used for your ladybird pin cushion, you can now progress to making some jolly bug bean bags, colourful ladybird seat cushions, or any other simple cushion shapes.

CREATING A BEAN BUG

You can use polka dot fabric for the top of your bug bean bag if you like, but why not use a cheery gingham fabric instead? With a head, underside, and wing crease made from black felt, your bug bean bag will still give the impression it's a ladybird, but you'll be able to indulge your creativity.

Make the bug bean bag in exactly the same way as you made the ladybird pin cushion (see pp.65–68), but when it comes to adding the stuffing, use bean-bag filling instead of wadding. You can buy

If you are feeling adventurous, you can decorate the front of your cushion with ribbon, upholstery or lace trim, buttons of various shapes, sizes, and colours, fabric puffs (see p.54), embroidery (see pp.56–59), or felt flowers (see pp.61–63). Just make sure that you always add your decoration to the front of the cushion before you sew the front and back together, and attach it very securely. Once the two are joined, it will be much more tricky to add your decoration.

If you don't yet feel quite ready to add this sort of decoration, why not simply make the front and back of your cushion from contrasting fabric for a reversible cushion? For instance, you could use a plain cotton fabric on one side and a small floral print or gingham on the other.

2

Build On It

Now you're ready to tackle the elephant in the room – the sewing machine! Machine-sewing will speed things up and broaden your range. Start with simple seams and end with homemade bias strips. With these techniques at your disposal you can sew a case for your eReader, a tea towel, an eco-friendly tote bag and some bunting to help you celebrate your new-learned skills. And to crown it all, try some upcycling: breathe new life into a discarded pillowcase by turning it into a child's dress.

In this section learn to make:

eReader Case
pp.84–89

Tea Towel
pp.96–100

Tote Bag
pp.106–111

Bunting
pp.116–120

How to **Sew Machine Stitches**

By now you should be feeling confident about your hand sewing skills, so it's time to get to grips with your sewing machine. Using a machine opens up a whole new world of sewing possibilities and speeds up the entire process. In no time at all you'll have made several useful items, for example a case for your eReader or tablet.

Securing machine stitches

The last thing you want is for your machine stitches to come undone and a seam to unravel. You can secure the stitches at the start and finish of the seam by hand, or by using the machine.

Tying the ends

This simple technique ensures your method of securing is as invisible as possible. On the back of the fabric, leave long top and bottom (bobbin) threads at the start and the end of your seam.

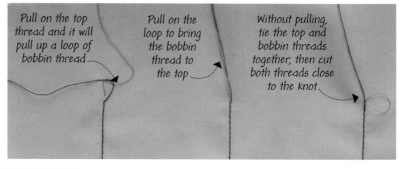

Pull on the top thread and it will pull up a loop of bobbin thread.....

Pull on the loop to bring the bobbin thread to the top .....

Without pulling, tie the top and bobbin threads together, then cut both threads close to the knot.....

Lock stitch

Some modern machines have a lock stitch button. Press this before you start and the needle will go up and down on the spot a few times to lock the first few stitches. The machine will then stop working, even with your foot on the pedal. Take the pressure off, then press down on it again to continue sewing a seam.

To finish, stop sewing, press the lock stitch button again and press the foot pedal. Now your last stitch will be locked too

Reverse stitch

Most machines have a reverse button. At the start of the seam, sew a few stitches forward. Then press the reverse button and holding it down, machine backwards over the first few stitches. Release the button and then continue forwards to the end of the seam.

At the end, press the reverse button again and machine backwards to secure the stitches

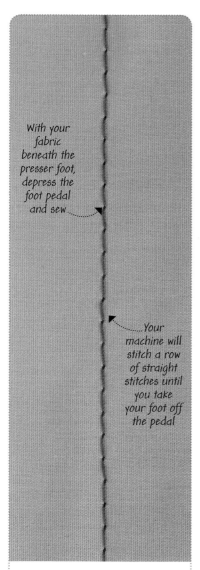

With your fabric beneath the presser foot, depress the foot pedal and sew

Your machine will stitch a row of straight stitches until you take your foot off the pedal

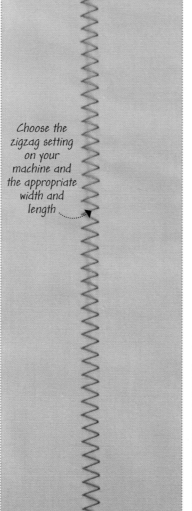

Choose the zigzag setting on your machine and the appropriate width and length

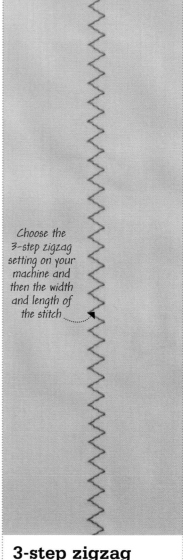

Choose the 3-step zigzag setting on your machine and then the width and length of the stitch

Straight stitches

This is a basic machine stitch for seams or topstitching. You can adjust the stitch length up to 4mm (⅛in) or even to 5mm (¼in) on some machines. The finer the fabric, the smaller your stitch length should be.

Zigzag

Use this stitch to neaten the raw edges of seams, for decoration, and for machine appliqué. You can adjust both the length and the width of the zigzag. If you want to appliqué, you'll need a short and narrow stitch.

3-step zigzag

This looks rather like a regular zigzag stitch, but each of these zigzags is made up of a number of small stitches. It's good for stitching stretchy fabrics, attaching elastic, and for neatening the edge of fabrics that fray easily.

How to **Make a Plain Seam**

Sewing a seam is what you do whenever you join two – or sometimes more – pieces of fabric together. A plain seam is not only the simplest type of seam, but also the most common and the most versatile. This makes it the best type of seam for a beginner to learn. Sew it using a straight stitch on your machine.

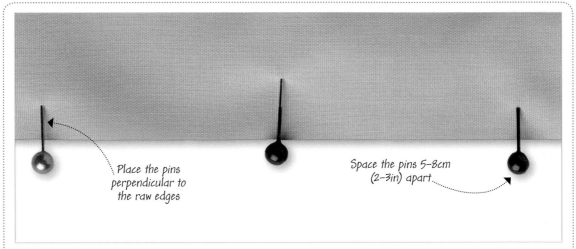

Place the pins perpendicular to the raw edges

Space the pins 5–8cm (2–3in) apart

1 Carefully pin your two pieces of fabric together, with the right sides facing each other. Place the pins perpendicular to the raw (unfinished) edges of the fabric. Space the pins evenly along the edge, making sure the two layers of fabric are lying flat.

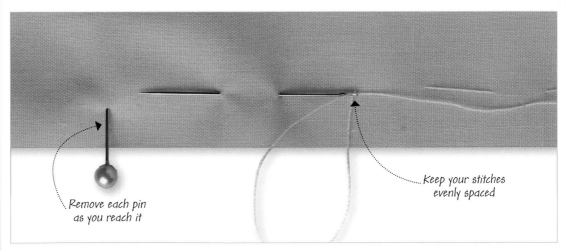

Remove each pin as you reach it

Keep your stitches evenly spaced

2 Stitch a row of tacking stitches (see p.36) through the layers of fabric and along the seamline, a little below where you want your machined seam to be. Remove the pins as you get to them so they will not be in the way when you machine stitch.

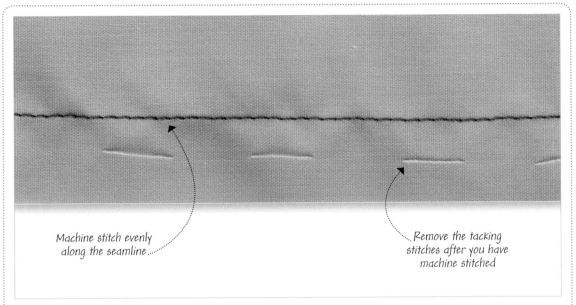

Machine stitch evenly along the seamline

Remove the tacking stitches after you have machine stitched

3 Using a straight stitch, lower the needle into the fabric using the balance wheel, then lower the presser foot. Stitch along the seamline using the seam guide on the needle plate to help you keep your stitches an even distance from the edges of the fabric. Secure the stitching at the start and end of the seam, then remove the tacking stitches.

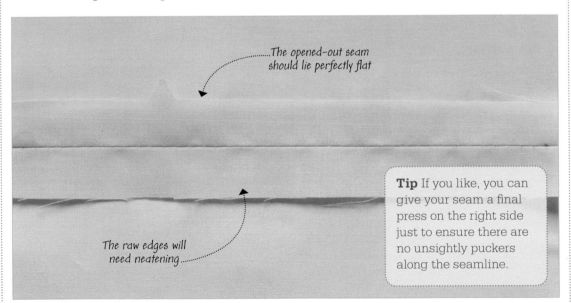

The opened-out seam should lie perfectly flat

The raw edges will need neatening

Tip If you like, you can give your seam a final press on the right side just to ensure there are no unsightly puckers along the seamline.

4 Open out the fabric. With the right side of your work face down, press the seam open along the line of stitches. You will end up with the seam running down the middle and the raw edges of the fabric lying flat on either side. See p.78 for how to neaten the raw edges.

How to **Neaten a Seam**

Once you've sewn your seam you'll need to neaten the raw edges to stop them from fraying. If you don't, the raw edges will fray with wear and tear and washing, putting strain on the stitching and leaving you with a split in your seam.

Overedge stitch

Worked with an overedge foot (see p.19), this stitch is similar to a zigzag but the raw edge of the fabric is finished with an overedge thread. This is a more secure way of preventing the fabric fraying. Set the stitch width to suit the fabric.

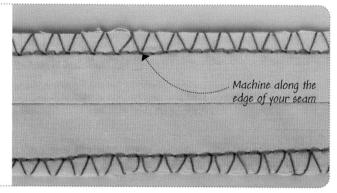

Machine along the edge of your seam

Don't trim away too much fabric

A pinked edge

This easy method of seam neatening is quick to perform and perfect for fabrics that don't fray too easily. All you have to do is cut along each of the raw edges using a pair of pinking shears. Make sure you trim away as little fabric as possible or you risk the edge fraying and the seam coming unstitched.

A stitch width of 2mm (¹⁄₁₆in) and a stitch length of 1.5mm (¹⁄₁₆in) works for most fabrics

Finish by trimming away the raw edge

A zigzagged edge

This type of finish works for all fabrics. Set your machine for a zigzag stitch. Place one raw edge of the seam under the presser foot, making sure you only have a single thickness of fabric there, then stitch a row of zigzags a little way in from the raw edge. Finish by trimming away the raw edge close to the zigzag stitches.

How to **Stitch a Corner**

There you are, merrily sewing a straight line, when suddenly you find that you have to turn a sharp corner. Turning a corner isn't as difficult as you may think, but you need to take care or you may end up with more of a curve than a right angle.

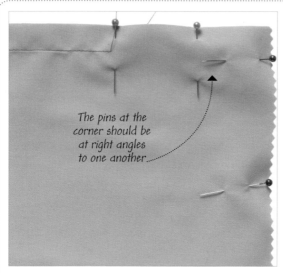

The pins at the corner should be at right angles to one another

Lift the presser foot to turn the fabric

1 Place the fabric pieces together, right side to right side. Pin along both seamlines, placing pins perpendicular to the fabric edge.

2 Stitch along the first seamline. At the corner, lower the needle, raise the presser foot, and turn the fabric 90 degrees.

Right-angled corner

Tip If you prefer, you can tack along the seamlines after pinning and remove the pins before you start to machine stitch.

3 Lower the presser foot again and continue stitching along the second seamline. You will end up with one seamline at a right angle to the other. When you turn the fabric inside out, wrong side to wrong side, your corner will have a sharp point.

How to **Attach Velcro™**

Velcro™ can be used to fasten everything from clothing to an eReader case. It consists of two strips, one with tiny hooks and the other with hairy loops. When the two are pressed together, they cling to each other firmly, but are easily pulled apart. Attaching Velcro™ is a simple process requiring only a straight machine stitch.

Pin the strips in place

Tip If you prefer, you can tack along the edges of each strip after pinning and remove the pins before you start to machine stitch.

1 Cut the Velcro™ to the required length and prise the two strips apart. Carefully pin the looped strip of Velcro™ to one layer of fabric and the hooked strip of Velcro™ to the other.

2 Using a straight stitch (see p.75), stitch right around the edges of each strip of Velcro™, turning at the corners (see p.79). Remove the pins after stitching.

How to **Attach Snap Fasteners**

Also known as snaps, poppers, and press studs, snap fasteners can make a good alternative to buttons. They are made of two parts: one with a ball-like protrusion that fits into a recess in the other. Choose metal snap fasteners for heavy fabrics and plastic ones for lightweight fabrics.

Attaching snaps

1

Tack each half of the snap in place with a couple of stitches through the holes

2

Attach the snap by stitching repeatedly through its holes and into the fabric

3

Remove the tacks when the snap is securely attached

Work your way round all the holes, making sure that your stitches don't show through on the right side

Alternative method

Plastic snap fasteners

These are usually either white or clear plastic and are normally square in shape. Attach them in exactly the same way as metal snap fasteners.

How to **Apply Fusible Interfacing**

An interfacing is a layer that is applied to fabric to reinforce it and give it extra strength, for example when adding structure to a tote bag, see pp.106–110. There are two types of interfacing: fusible and non-fusible. Fusible interfacings, which are backed with an adhesive activated by heat, are the easiest to use.

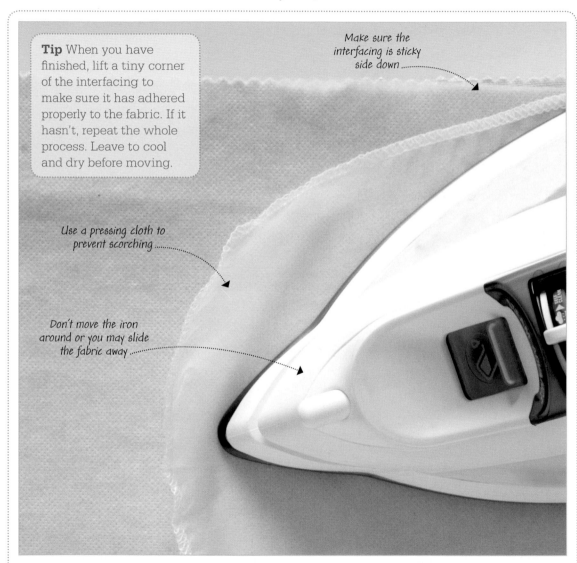

Tip When you have finished, lift a tiny corner of the interfacing to make sure it has adhered properly to the fabric. If it hasn't, repeat the whole process. Leave to cool and dry before moving.

Make sure the interfacing is sticky side down

Use a pressing cloth to prevent scorching

Don't move the iron around or you may slide the fabric away

Using a steam iron set to the correct temperature, lay the fabric on the ironing board, wrong side up. Make sure there are no wrinkles in it. Place the interfacing sticky side down on the fabric and cover with a damp pressing cloth. Hold the iron in place for about 10 seconds for lightweight fabric and 15 seconds for heavier fabric.

Fusible interfacings

Woven fusible interfacings are designed for use with woven fabric

Woven

Like woven fabric, woven fusible interfacing has a lengthwise and a crosswise grain. Always use a woven interfacing if you are working with a woven fabric and make sure you cut the interfacing on the same grain as the fabric.

Lightweight woven

This delicate, almost sheer, woven fusible interfacing is suitable for all light to medium-weight fabrics. It can be difficult to cut out as it has a tendency to stick to the scissors.

Lightweight woven fusible interfacings are designed for use with lighter woven fabrics

Non-woven

Made by bonding fibres together, non-woven fusible interfacing doesn't have a grain so it's easier to cut out than a woven interfacing. Another plus is the fact that it does not fray. It is a good, all-purpose interfacing.

Choose the appropriate weight of non-woven fusible interfacing for your project

Non-fusible interfacing

This interfacing comes in various types and weights. The most commonly used is non-woven, shown here. Hold all non-fusible interfacings in place by pinning them, then tacking to the wrong side of the fabric, before machine stitching. Remove the tacking stitches after you've sewn.

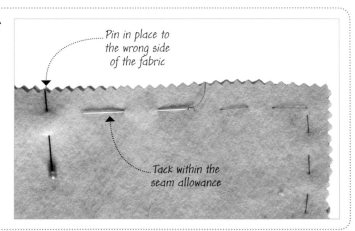

Pin in place to the wrong side of the fabric

Tack within the seam allowance

Make an eReader Case

There are plenty of eReader cases on the market but it's so much nicer to have a homemade one. Not only is it more unique, but it adds a low-tech touch to your high-tech piece of kit. Well padded with wadding, this case will protect your eReader for years to come.

You will need:
Templates from p.178 • Fabric: floral outer and plain lining • Interfacing • Sheet wadding
Fabric scissors • Velcro™: 6cm (2½in) • Iron and ironing board • Pins
Sewing machine • Needle • Thread

1 Cut out all the pieces of fabric and interfacing required for the eReader case and its tab, using the templates on pp.178–179. Use the template to cut the strips of Velcro™. Begin by preparing the eReader tab: apply the fusible interfacing to the wrong side of the tab lining fabric.

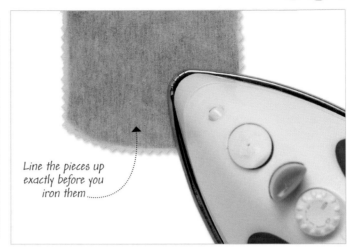

Line the pieces up exactly before you iron them.......

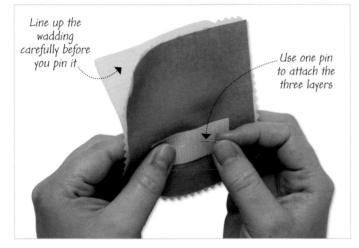

Line up the wadding carefully before you pin it....

.... Use one pin to attach the three layers

2 Attach the tab wadding to the interfaced side of the tab and the hooked strip of Velcro™ to the right side of the tab using one pin. Position the Velcro™ about 2cm (¾in) from the top of the tab, centred horizontally.

Tip Attach the Velcro™ so that the hooked half is on the tab, and the soft half is attached to the case.

3 Machine sew the Velcro™ in place by sewing a line of straight stitches along all four edges. Lay the outer fabric of the tab on top, with the right side facing down – the Velcro™ should be sandwiched in the middle. Pin in place then machine along three sides using a straight stitch. Leave the bottom open. Trim the excess fabric away from the corners then turn the tab right side out and iron flat.

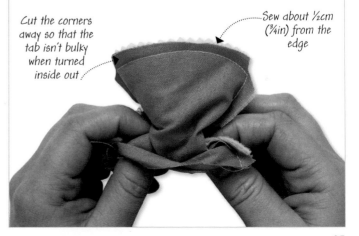

Cut the corners away so that the tab isn't bulky when turned inside out ...

Sew about ½cm (¾in) from the edge

5 Now make the lining for the case. Iron interfacing to the wrong side of each piece of lining. Place the pieces together, lining inwards, interfacing outwards. Pin together along two of the long sides and across one short side, leaving a gap of 8cm (3in) in the middle of the short side. You will need this gap to turn the case to the right side in Step 12. Machine in place about 1cm (½in) from the edge. Remove the pins as you go.

Leave a gap in the bottom

Your stitches should form a rectangle on the Velcro™

6 Pin the hairy looped strip of Velcro™ in place on the front outer piece. Position it 2.5cm (1in) from the top and centre it horizontally. Check it against the tab to make sure the two pieces of Velcro™ will line up. Machine sew it in place, using a straight stitch around its four sides.

Remember Ensure that you sew neat right angles at the corners.

7 Place the two outer pieces of fabric, right sides together. Sandwich these between the two pieces of wadding, and pin all four layers together along the bottom edge and the two sides.

Careful! Doublecheck which end of the case is the top before pinning the layers in place – you must leave the top unpinned.

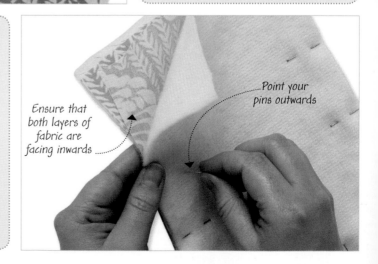

Ensure that both layers of fabric are facing inwards

Point your pins outwards

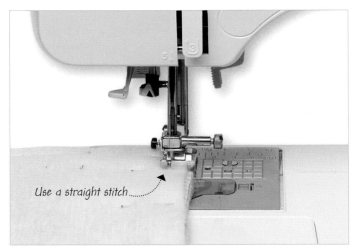

Use a straight stitch

8 Machine the four layers of fabric together along the three pinned sides. Sew about 1cm (½in) from the edge of the fabric. Remove all the pins. Using fabric scissors, trim the two corners by cutting away a small triangle.

Tip Trimming the corners will mean that they turn inside out cleanly and won't be bulky.

9 Turn the lining the right way out. Place the tab in position, with the Velcro™ facing down. The tab must be centred and straight, with the edge aligned with the top of the case – measure it to make sure it is in the right place, then pin. Slide the lining inside the external layer – which is still inside out. The tab should now be touching the external layer of the case that doesn't have Velcro™ on it.

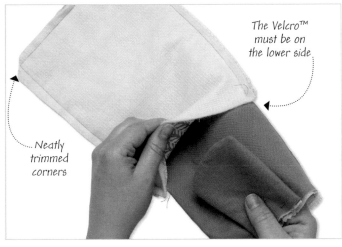

The Velcro™ must be on the lower side

Neatly trimmed corners

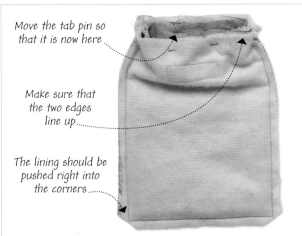

Move the tab pin so that it is now here

Make sure that the two edges line up

The lining should be pushed right into the corners

10 Hold the tab in place then remove the pin and reinsert it so that the tab is sandwiched between the two layers – otherwise the pin will become trapped inside the lining. Ensure that the top of the outer and inner layers are lined up then pin them together. It is vital to get these to line up as closely as possible, so that the seam sits on the top edge of the join once the case is the right way out.

11 Machine sew the two layers together, working your way around the rim of the bag, keeping the two layers aligned as closely as possible. You may need to manipulate the fabric to get it into the right position. This is quite fiddly – a little wobble is hard to avoid. If your line looks wonky you can re-sew it – see opposite for a tip on how to correct this.

Sew about 1cm (½in) from the edge of the fabric

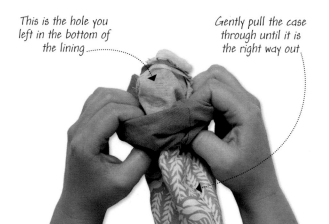

This is the hole you left in the bottom of the lining

Gently pull the case through until it is the right way out

12 Once you are happy that you have sewn a straight line across the top, remove all the pins and pull the lining fabric back out towards you – the linked pieces will both be inside out. Using the hole you left in the bottom of the lining, gently pull the fabric through to turn the case inside out.

13 Poke the corners out carefully so that they are nice and square – carefully use a knitting needle to get right into the corners. Iron the case flat and then slip stitch up the hole. When you are finished, push the lining into place inside the case, and your eReader case is ready to use.

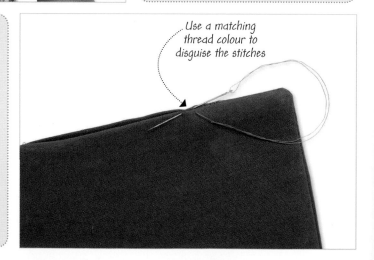

Use a matching thread colour to disguise the stitches

The perfect **eReader Case**

This lovely padded case will keep your eReader safe from harm – for a really polished product, ensure that your corners are neat and your Velcro™ strips line up.

Sharp, neat corners

The Velcro™ pieces line up exactly

The seam should sit on the top edge

Straight edges

If you didn't manage to get the line along the top of the case completely straight, don't panic. It can be very fiddly to manipulate so many layers of material at once. Use a ruler and pencil to draw a line below your wonky line of stitches, and sew carefully along this instead. When you turn the case inside out again, it will be this lower line that will form the shape of the case. It is too tricky to try and draw this line before you've sewn, so keep this trick up your sleeve in case you need it.

Neat fastening

It is important to make sure that your tab is in the right position so that your Velcro™ pieces line up. Make sure that you pin the Velcro™ exactly central on both the tab and the case. Position them about 2.5cm (1in) from the top edge of the case, and 2cm (¾in) from the top of the tab. That way the two will align once all the pieces have been sewn together.

Also learn to make ▶ ▶ ▶

Phone Case and Tablet Cover

Once you've made a case for your eReader you won't want to stop there, so why not create a protective padded case for your phone and tablet as well? There are a number of different closures that you could choose from – you could use a Velcro™ tab as you did for the eReader case, or experiment with ribbons or a button fastening.

CREATING A PHONE CASE

As every phone is a different size there is no template supplied for this project. You'll need to measure your phone and add 3cm (1½in) to the width and height. Cut the outer fabric, lining, wadding, and interfacing to this size. If you wish to decorate the case with an appliqué heart, such as the one shown here, you must sew it on before you assemble the case. Cut out your heart shape from your chosen fabric, pin it to the case, and then sew around the outside edge using a zigzag stitch.

You will make the case in exactly the same way as the eReader, Steps 5–13 (see pp.86–88), but you will need to adapt the instructions in order to create this button fastening. Cut a loop of elastic, about 12cm (5in) long. Do not make and attach a tab but instead, at Step 10, when you pin the case to the lining, insert the looped elastic between the case and the lining at the back. Centre the loop horizontally, overlapping the ends of the loop by about 2.5cm (1in) to ensure they are secured firmly by the stitching. Pin in place then continue with Step 11. Once you have turned the case the right way out and ironed it flat, sew a button onto the front of the case (see p.39) to align with the elastic. To create the gingham band: measure the width of the case then double this to cover both sides. Cut a strip of fabric 1cm (½in) longer than this and your chosen depth. Fold the edges under on all four sides and iron flat. Pin the band in place and then slip stitch in place by hand (see p.37).

Tip Your elastic will hold better if you use a button with a shank on the back, rather than a flat type.

CREATING A TABLET COVER

To create a tablet cover, measure your device and add 3cm (1½in) to the width and height. Cut the outer fabric, lining, wadding, and interfacing to this size and cut two lengths of ribbon, 30cm (12in) long. Choose a sturdy fabric if you are likely to be frequently slipping the case in and out of your bag as you travel, and consider investigating different thicknesses of wadding, so that you can ensure that your tablet will be safely cushioned. Again, you will make this in the same way as the eReader case, following Steps 5–13 (see pp.86–88). Do not make and attach a tab but instead, at Step 10, slide a length of ribbon between the case and the lining at both the front and the back. Overlap their ends by about 5cm (2in) to ensure they are secured firmly by the stitching and pin them in place. Ensure they are pinned centrally and that they line up – pinch the top edges of the cover together to check. Continue with Step 11, taking care not to sew over the ribbon pieces or get them tangled. For decoration, sew another piece of ribbon, in a contrasting colour, around the top of the bag – sew along the top and the bottom to secure it.

How to **Make Hems and Hanging Loops**

We associate hems with the bottoms of skirts or trousers, but they have many other uses. Once you've mastered machine- and hand-finished hems, you'll be able to edge tea towels, napkins, table runners, tablecloths, and other similar items. You'll also be able to make loops to hang up all your neatly finished tea towels.

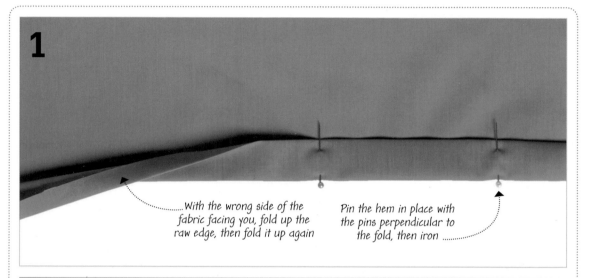

1

......With the wrong side of the fabric facing you, fold up the raw edge, then fold it up again

Pin the hem in place with the pins perpendicular to the fold, then iron ....

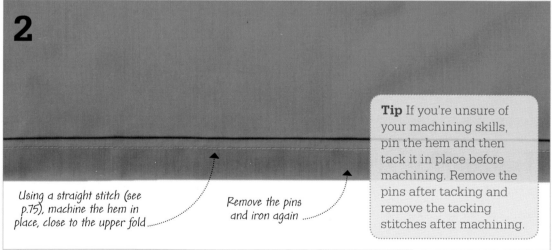

2

Using a straight stitch (see p.75), machine the hem in place, close to the upper fold ....

Remove the pins and iron again ....

Tip If you're unsure of your machining skills, pin the hem and then tack it in place before machining. Remove the pins after tacking and remove the tacking stitches after machining.

Double-turn hem

This machine-made hem is one of the simplest to master. It adds some weight to the edge as the fabric is doubled over. The final fold should be exactly where you want your hem to be, so check you have enough fabric to fold over twice in order to achieve this.

1

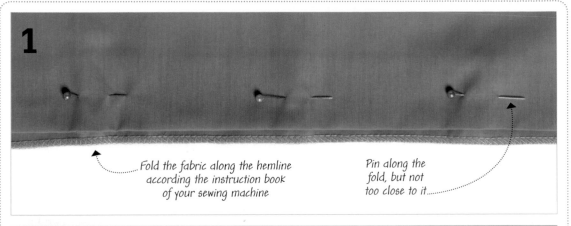

Fold the fabric along the hemline
according the instruction book
of your sewing machine

Pin along the
fold, but not
too close to it

2

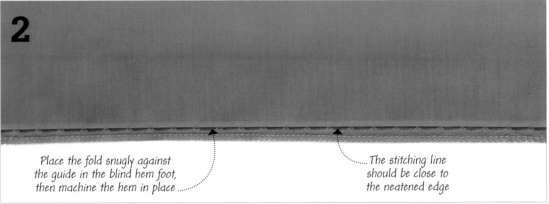

Place the fold snugly against
the guide in the blind hem foot,
then machine the hem in place

The stitching line
should be close to
the neatened edge

3

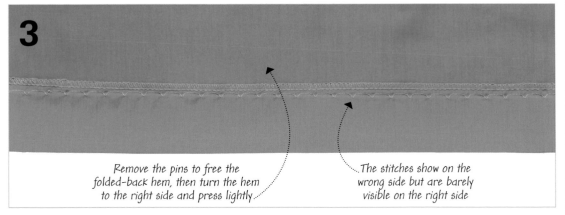

Remove the pins to free the
folded-back hem, then turn the hem
to the right side and press lightly

The stitches show on the
wrong side but are barely
visible on the right side

Blind hem

This machine-made hem only has a single
turn. You will need to use the blind hem foot
on your sewing machine. Before you start,
neaten the raw edge of the fabric so it doesn't
fray. You can use a pinked or zigzagged edge
(see p.78) or an overlocker (see p.20).

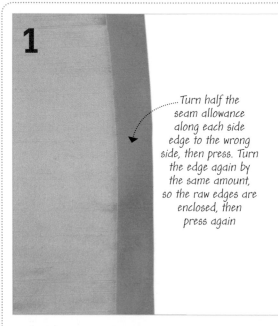

1

...Turn half the seam allowance along each side edge to the wrong side, then press. Turn the edge again by the same amount, so the raw edges are enclosed, then press again

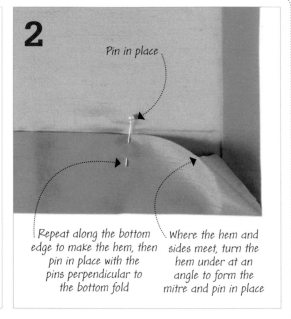

2

Pin in place

Repeat along the bottom edge to make the hem, then pin in place with the pins perpendicular to the bottom fold

Where the hem and sides meet, turn the hem under at an angle to form the mitre and pin in place

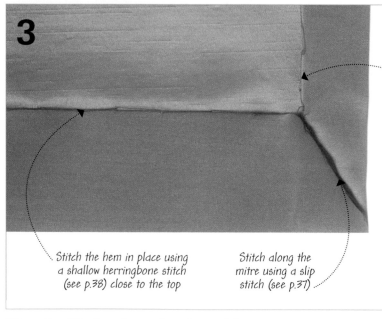

3

Stitch the sides in place using the same herringbone stitch

Stitch the hem in place using a shallow herringbone stitch (see p.38) close to the top

Stitch along the mitre using a slip stitch (see p.37)

Tip If the fabric is too bulky at the mitre, before you do any final stitching, open the mitre out and trim away some of the excess fabric. Fold the mitre back into place.

Hand-stitched and mitred hem

Use a hand-stitched hem when you don't want any stitching to show on the right side. Combine it with properly mitred edges and you'll have a neat-looking, professional finish when hemming the sides and bottom edges of curtains.

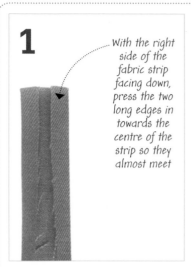

1 With the right side of the fabric strip facing down, press the two long edges in towards the centre of the strip so they almost meet

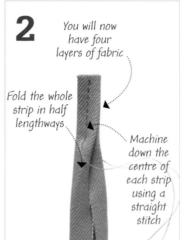

2 You will now have four layers of fabric

Fold the whole strip in half lengthways

Machine down the centre of each strip using a straight stitch

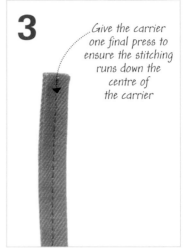

3 Give the carrier one final press to ensure the stitching runs down the centre of the carrier

Machine-stitched loops

You can make fabric loops almost any length or width, for uses as diverse as hanging your tea towels (see pp.96–100) to making straps for a child's dress (see pp.124–129). When you cut your fabric strips, bear in mind that you'll fold them so they end up a quarter of their original width. You should also allow a bit of extra length so that you can turn the ends up.

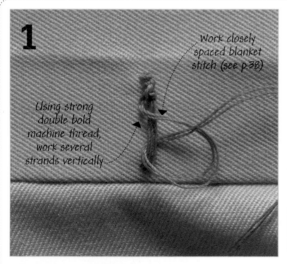

1 Work closely spaced blanket stitch (see p.38)

Using strong double bold machine thread, work several strands vertically

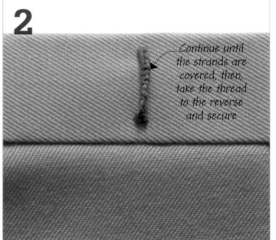

2 Continue until the strands are covered, then, take the thread to the reverse and secure

Hand-stitched loops

This simple style of loop is constructed using strong machine thread, stitched over and over on itself for strength. You could use this loop as an alternative for hanging up a tea towel, but it will not hold as much weight as a machine-stitched loop. Make sure that your initial vertical strands are long enough to hang over your hook.

Make a Tea Towel

Our cheery apple print tea towel brightens up the kitchen and makes drying the dishes far less of a chore. It's one of the simplest machine-sewn projects you could possibly tackle, so why stop at making only one? A homemade tea towel makes a great present for a friend.

You will need:
Fabric: printed cotton, 50 x 75cm (20 x 30in); hanging loop fabric, 13 x 4.5cm (5in x 1 ¾in)
Fabric scissors • Iron and ironing board • Pins • Sewing machine • Thread

1 First, make your fabric loop. Fold the fabric rectangle lengthways in half and crease a line down the centre. Fold the edges inwards to meet this line and iron it into place. Then press these folded edges inwards to create one four-ply strip of fabric. Pin the fabric to prevent it moving, and machine stitch along the open edge using a straight stitch.

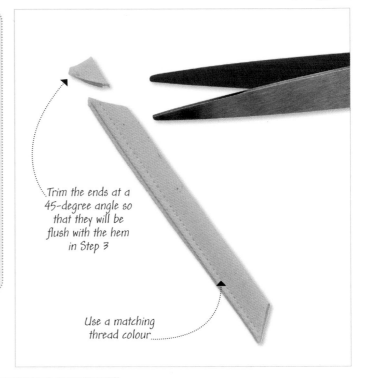

Trim the ends at a 45-degree angle so that they will be flush with the hem in Step 3

Use a matching thread colour

Fold over the two short edges first, then repeat on the two long sides

Fold twice, tucking the raw edge under

2 On one of the short sides of the tea towel fabric, measure 2.5cm (1in), fold it over, and iron it in place. Repeat on the opposite short edge, then fold these edges under again, so that the hem is now 1.25cm (½in) deep and the raw edge of the fabric is enclosed. Iron again and pin in place. Repeat this process on the two long edges, pinning the corners into place as you do so. Manipulate the fabric with your fingers to ensure that the corners sit flat.

3 Decide which corner you want your hanging loop in. Pin it securely across the corner, tucking it right into the hem. You may have to unpin a bit of each hem to make space for the ends of the loop. Pin again when the loop is in position.

Tip If your fabric has a pattern on it with an obvious "right way up", make sure you attach your loop to one of the top corners.

Push the hanging loop right under the hem

The corners should be neatly flattened before sewing

Position the pins pointing outwards so that you can easily sew over them

4 Rather than sewing around the edge of the tea towel in one go, you need to sew the two short edges first and then sew the two longer sides – that way the fabric is less likely to twist as you sew. Use a straight stitch and a matching thread colour.

Tip Try to get your line of machine stitching to run straight down the middle of the hem. Use the guides on the needle plate to help you.

5 When you come to the corner with the hanging loop, sew as slowly as you can, to ensure that you have stitched through both the hem and the ends of the loop. You don't want your hanging loop to give way when you use it.

Tip For added strength, you can machine a second time over the the hanging loop at the points where it slips under the hem.

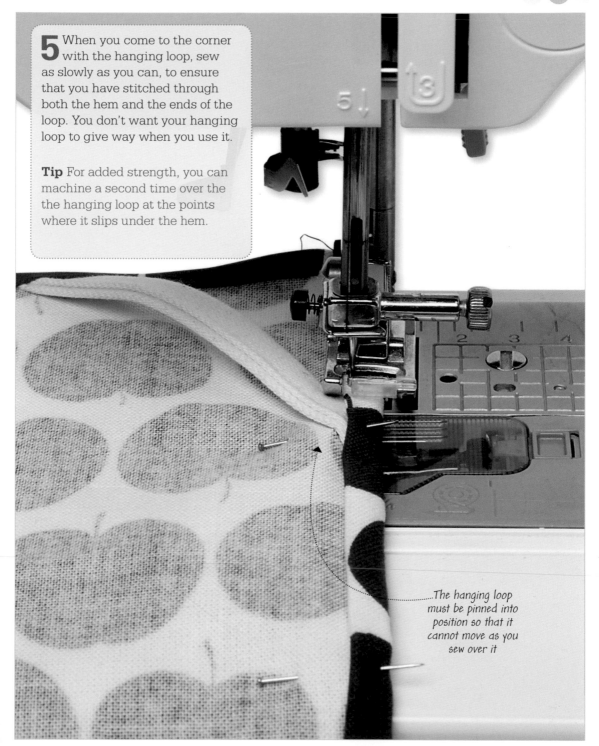

The hanging loop must be pinned into position so that it cannot move as you sew over it

The perfect **Tea Towel**

This simple project can brighten up your kitchen and would make a perfect gift for family or friends – just make sure the hanging loop is firmly attached.

The tea towel forms a symmetrical shape when folded

The pattern is at right angles to the edge of the fabric

The hanging loop is firmly secured

Straight patterns

If you are using a patterned fabric with stripes or lines of shapes, such as the apple print used here, cut along the fabric's selvedges (see p.22) to ensure that the edges of the tea towel and the pattern are parallel or at right angles to each other.

Secure hook

If the hanging loop has been pushed right under the double hem it should be firmly attached. If it starts to come loose, secure it with some hand stitches – it will be too untidy to unpick the machine-stitched sides.

Symmetrical shape

Check your tea towel's symmetry by folding it in on itself. If the shape is not perfectly rectangular it may be because the fabric was ironed at a slightly incorrect angle before sewing. In reality this isn't really a big problem, but doublecheck this the next time you make a tea towel, or if you make napkins, a table runner, or a table cloth (see pp.101–103). Hemming the top and bottom edges before sewing up the two sides also helps to ensure that the fabric remains square.

Also learn to make ▶ ▶ ▶

Napkins

Why not add a touch of elegance to your table by sewing yourself a set of napkins? Not only do they look far nicer than paper serviettes, but they are much more eco-friendly and will last you for years. Choose one fabric and make a matching set, or make them from complementary colours and patterns – the choice is yours.

CREATING NAPKINS

Napkins are really simple to make. You make them in the same way as tea towels but without the hanging loop. Choose cotton fabric that is relatively thick but also soft to the touch. You could make your napkins to any size you want, but the ones shown here measure 50 x 50cm (20 x 20in). Cut your squares of fabric, ensuring that the edges are parallel to or at right angles to the selvedges (see p.22).

Turn two opposite edges over by 2cm (¾in) and iron them flat. Tuck the raw edges under and into the fold and then iron flat again so that the

hems now measure about 1cm (½in). Pin the hems into place, spacing the pins every 5cm (2in), positioning them perpendicular to the fabric. Repeat this on the other two edges, folding the fabric neatly in place at the corners. Machine sew two opposite edges first, secure the thread and then sew the other two opposite edges. Use a straight machine stitch, and sew as close to the edge of the hem as you can.

Tip Why not personalize your napkins with some embroidery stitches (see pp.56–59) or some appliqué shapes?

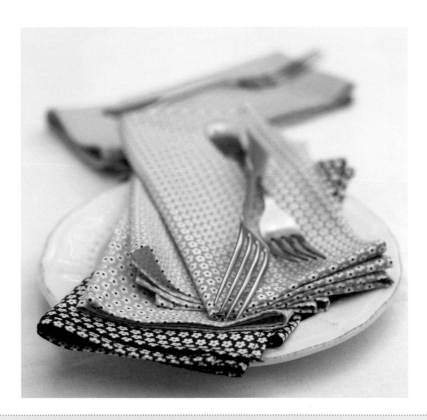

Table Runner and Tablecloth

Once you've mastered making tea towels and napkins, complete the set with a tablecloth and table runner. Choose hardwearing cotton, as they will need to withstand a lot of wear and tear.

CREATING A TABLE RUNNER

This project uses the same simple techniques as the tea towel but features panels of contrasting material and decorative trimming along the ends. For this project you will need a length of patterned fabric for the main part of the runner, 110 x 35cm (3½ft x 14in), two plain panels, 6 x 35 cm (2½ x 14in), and two pieces of trimming, 35cm (14in) long.

To insert the plain panels, cut off 8cm (3in) from each end of the patterned fabric and put these pieces to one side. Lay the remaining patterned fabric wrong side down and place a band of plain fabric wrong side up on top of it so the long edge of the plain band aligns with the cut edge of the patterned fabric. Pin in place and using a straight stitch, sew the two together 1cm (½in) from the edges. Open up the joined pieces of fabric and lay them right side down, then place one of the spare pieces of patterned fabric to the free edge of the plain band, wrong side to wrong side. Pin in place and stitch as you did on the other edge of the band.

Repeat at the other end of the patterned fabric to insert the second plain panel. Iron all the seams flat. If one fabric is lighter than the other, make sure that the lighter fabric overlaps the darker one. Create a double hem along the two short sides (see p.92), then repeat along the two long sides. To finish, pin your trimming to the underside of the two short ends, and sew it carefully into place.

CREATING A TABLECLOTH

Make your tablecloth to fit your table – simply measure the table and add about 30cm (12in) to the length and width so that the fabric can overhang on all sides. Decide how long or short you want your panels of patterned fabric on each end to be and then work out how much plain fabric you will need to go between them, allowing about 6cm (2½in) for making the seams. Cut your fabric to size, ensuring that the widths of both the patterned and plain fabrics are the same. Sew the pieces of fabric together using the method described above for making the table runner, then iron all the seams flat.

Make a double hem along the two short sides (see p.92), then repeat on the other two, so that all four sides are neatly hemmed. To decorate, sew a length of ribbon over the join between the fabrics – this will give a really neat finish. Turn the ends of the ribbon under at either end so that there are no raw edges on show. To ensure that the ribbon lies flat, sew along the top edge first and once you reach the end, sew back along the bottom edge. Finish by machining the turned-under ends.

Tip Why not match the coloured panels on the table cloth with a set of napkins?

How to **Make a Simple Pocket**

The key to getting a professional look when you attach a pocket to your project is to take care when you position it. Nothing shows up an amateur sewer more than lopsided work. To make a pocket, simply cut a piece of fabric to the size and shape you want, neaten the raw edge with a zigzag or overedge stitch, then fold 1cm (½in) of fabric to the wrong side, all around the edge. If your pocket has curved corners, sew running stitch around the curve, then pull it gently to gather the fabric up. At the corners, fold the fabric under and secure it neatly with a few stitches. Iron the pocket flat and into shape, then it is ready to attach.

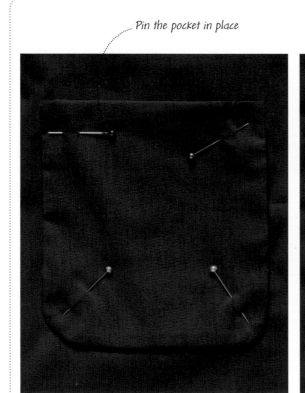

... Pin the pocket in place

Keep your tacking stitches close to the edge of the pocket ....

1 On the right side of your garment, mark where the top edges of your pocket should go using a chalk pencil (see p.13). Then place the wrong side of the completed pocket on the right side of the garment, aligning the top edge of the pocket with your marks. Use pins to hold the pocket in place.

2 You need to make sure the pocket stays in position while you machine sew it in place. Tack from one top corner of the pocket right the way around the pocket to the other top corner, keeping close to the finished edge. Remember to leave the top of the pocket open. Remove all your pins after you have finished.

Tip If you are nervous about sewing such a visible line of stitches, go very slowly, especially around the corners.

Machine stitch around the pocket as close to the edge as you can

Hold the pocket in place with pins but remove them as you work your way round

Don't forget to leave the top edge of your pocket open

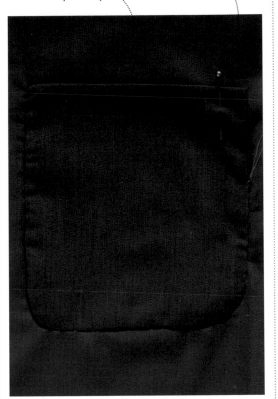

3 With the pocket face up and using a straight stitch, machine about 1mm (¹⁄₃₂in) from the edge of the pocket, next to your tacking stitches. You should end up with a neat line of topstitching round the sides and bottom of the pocket. Remove the tacking stitches and press.

Alternative method

Attaching the pocket by hand

If you don't want visible topstitching on your pocket, you can attach it to your project by hand instead. Follow Steps 1–2, then use a slip stitch (see p.37) through the folded edge of the pocket. Use a matching thread colour so that the stitches are completely hidden. Don't pull the thread too tightly as you work or the pocket will wrinkle.

Make a Tote Bag

Want to stand out in the crowd as you do your weekly shop – and boost your environmentalist street-cred at the same time? Then make this irresistible, easy-to-sew tote bag. You could push the boat out and decorate your finished bag with a homemade felt flower.

You will need:

Fabric: two pieces of floral fabric, 33 x 28cm (13 x 11in); two pieces of plain fabric, 33 x 11.5cm (13 x 4 ½in) lining fabric, 70 x 33cm (27½ x 13in); two pieces of interfacing, 70 x 33cm (27½ x 13in) two pieces of strap fabric, 56 x 6.5cm (22 x 2½in); two lengths of webbing, 56 x 4cm (22 x 1½in) Ribbon: 33cm (13in) • Fabric scissors • Pins • Sewing machine • Thread Iron and ironing board • Needle

1 Cut out your fabric and lay the pieces out to make sure that the lengths of floral fabric, the plain fabric, the lining fabric, and the panels of interfacing are all exactly the same width.

Tip Webbing is a strong tape-like fabric that is used for strengthening items like straps or handles. If you are unable to find any, you can substitute it with stiff interfacing.

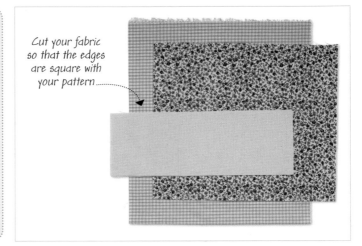

Cut your fabric so that the edges are square with your pattern....

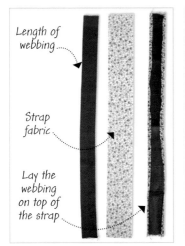

Length of webbing.....

Strap fabric.

Lay the webbing on top of the strap.

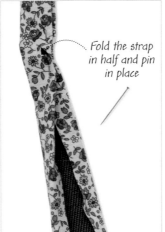

.... Fold the strap in half and pin in place

2 To create the tote straps, fold each long side of both pieces of strap fabric in by 1cm (½in) and iron in place. Lay the webbing or interfacing along the centre of the straps, tucked under the folded edges. Fold each strap in half lengthways and pin. Turn up 5mm (¼in) at the ends of each strap, to finish them neatly. Machine stitch along the straps, close to the open edge, using a straight stitch.

3 Next, join the floral and plain fabrics to make the front and back of the tote. With the right sides together, pin one short edge of each floral length to the long edge of each plain piece. Using a straight stitch, machine sew the floral fabric to the plain fabric, 1cm (½in) from the raw edges. Repeat with the other pieces of floral and plain fabric.

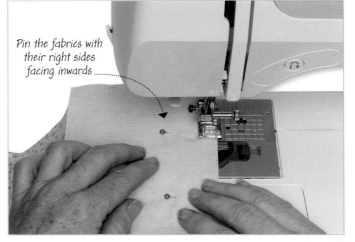

Pin the fabrics with their right sides facing inwards.........

4 Remove all the pins and place each piece of seamed fabric with the right side face down. Iron along the seams, pressing them apart. Iron fusible interfacing onto the back of your two seamed pieces.

Remember It's important to get the seams as flat as you can, so that the seamed fabric feels like one continuous piece.

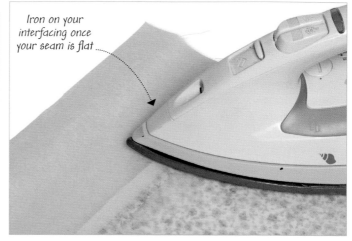

Iron on your interfacing once your seam is flat

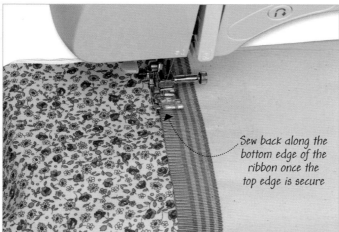

Sew back along the bottom edge of the ribbon once the top edge is secure

5 Choose which piece of fabric is to be the front of your tote and pin the ribbon along the seam joining the floral and plain fabrics. Machine stitch the ribbon in place using a straight stitch and thread in a matching colour.

Tip To keep the ribbon flat, sew along one long edge first, then go back and sew along the other.

6 Lay the interfaced front and back on top of each other, right sides together. Pin around the two long sides and the bottom, leaving the top edge open. Machine around the three pinned sides about 1cm (½in) from the edge of the fabric. Remove the pins.

Careful! Make sure you form neat right angles as you sew around the corners (see p.79).

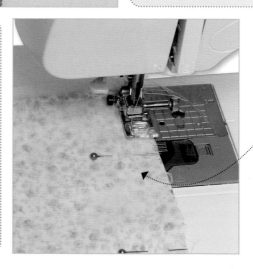

Machine sew your two outer pieces together

7 Using sharp fabric scissors, trim away the excess fabric from the corners at an angle. Leave about 5mm (¼in) between the stitches and the edge of the fabric. This will ensure that your corners are neat when the bag is turned the right way out. If you don't trim the fabric away, the corners will look bulky.

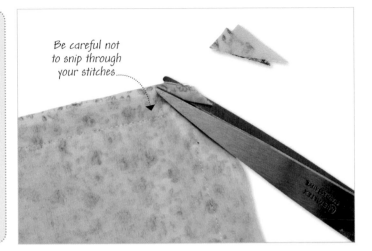

Be careful not to snip through your stitches ⋯⋯

8 Place the two pieces of lining fabric right sides together. Pin along the two long sides and along one short edge, leaving a gap of 13cm (5in) in the middle of this edge – you will use the gap to turn your bag the right way out in Step 11. Machine around the pinned sides as in Step 6.

Remember Once the thread is secure, trim the excess fabric from the corners (see Step 7).

9 Turn the lining the right way out. With the outer bag still inside out, slip the lining bag into it until its top edge is in line with the top edge of the outer bag. Pin the open edge of the bag to the open edge of the lining.

Careful! It's important that the two top edges line up so that the finished seam sits on the very top of the opening when you turn the bag to the right side.

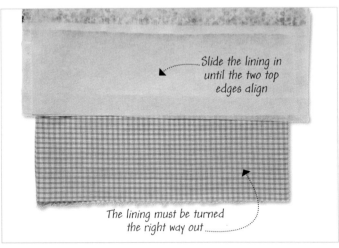

⋯Slide the lining in until the two top edges align

The lining must be turned the right way out ⋯⋯

10 Machine stitch the open edge of the bag to the open edge of the lining about 1cm (½in) from the edge of the fabric. Take care not to stitch all the layers together. You will need to manipulate the fabric to get it into the correct position under the presser foot.

Careful! Sew around the edge of the bag, not through all the layers.

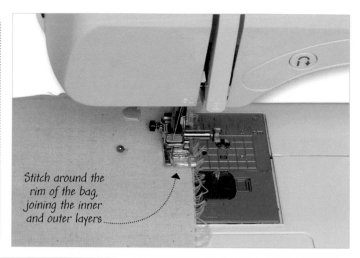

Stitch around the rim of the bag, joining the inner and outer layers

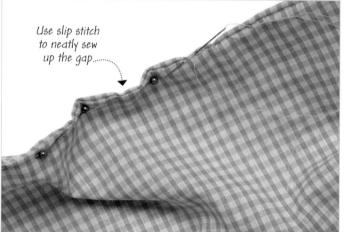

Use slip stitch to neatly sew up the gap

11 Remove all the pins. You now have two bags joined together at the top. Pull the lining out of the bag – the joined pieces will both be inside out. Gently pull the bag through the gap in the stitching that you left when you sewed up the lining in Step 8. The bag will now be the right way out. Use a knitting needle to carefully poke out the corners so they are nice and square. Use slip stitch to close the gap in the lining.

12 Push the lining into place inside the bag and iron around the top of the bag to ensure that the lining lies flat and that you have a sharp seam. Topstitch a row of machine stitches around the top of the bag, about ½cm (¼in) from the edge. This will ensure that the lining stays put. Finally, position the two straps, with the bottom of each end 7cm (3in) from the edge of the bag. Pin in place then machine into position.

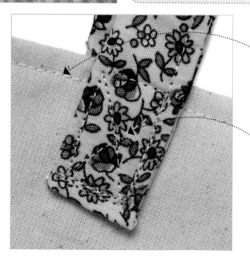

Add a finishing line of stitches using matching thread

This rectangle of stitches will ensure the straps are secure

The perfect **Tote Bag**

Tote bags are easy to make and useful to have – a lined version like this can carry a substantial amount of weight. Just make sure that you attach the straps securely.

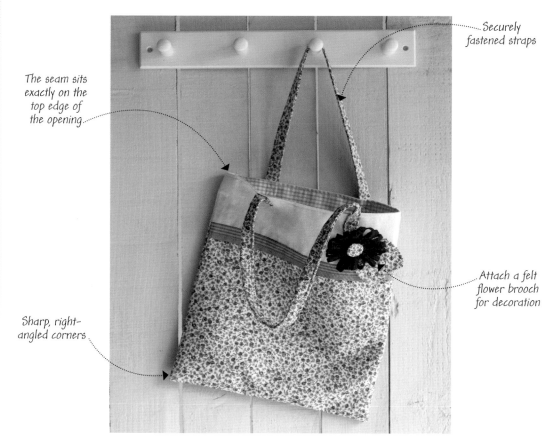

Securely fastened straps

The seam sits exactly on the top edge of the opening

Attach a felt flower brooch for decoration

Sharp, right-angled corners

Sharp corners

Your bag should be a neat rectangular shape and the corners should be sharp. Ensure that you sew precise right angles when you make the corners, and cut away any excess fabric so that the corners look neat.

Secure straps

The straps should be securely attached to your tote so that you can carry heavy items such as books or groceries without worrying that they will give way. Test after you sew them to check that they are secure enough. If not, machine over the stitches a second time.

Flattened, smooth fabric

Your bag should be smooth and flat, with no bulky seams. Iron the bag to flatten the seams and corners and to ensure that the lining lies flat along its top edge.

Also learn to make ▶ ▶ ▶

Add Handles and Pockets

If you want to make a tote that stands out from the crowd, why not personalize one? It's very easy to add leather handles or coloured pockets – both of which will make your bag uniquely yours. Shop around online and in department stores to see what you can find. Don't be afraid to mismatch styles and colours.

ADDING HANDLES

These smart leather handles and others like them are available to buy from craft shops and over the internet. Make your tote bag following Steps 1–11 on pp.106–110, then simply machine sew these handles onto the outside of the bag using a size 120 needle and strong machine thread.

Tip Straps like those shown opposite are sewn in place between the outer bag and the lining. To make, adapt the steps on pp.106–109. At the end of Step 9, slip each end of the straps between the outer bag and the lining, sliding them in so that about 2.5cm (1in) is sandwiched. Pin in place then continue with Step 10, machine-stitching the straps in position. For extra strength, you can machine over the ends of the straps a second time.

ADDING POCKETS

A splash of colour in the form of a useful pocket or two can perk up the appearance of an otherwise run-of-the-mill tote. Pockets are incredibly simple to make. Before you put your tote together, cut rectangles of fabric for your pockets making them about 1cm (½in) larger all round than the size you want them to be. Don't be afraid to mismatch colours and sizes. Fold 1cm (½in) over on the top and bottom of the rectangle and iron in place. Repeat on the other two edges. All you need to do now is position the pocket on the front of your tote – making sure that it isn't wonky – and pin it in place. Machine stitch neatly along the bottom and two sides, then make the tote following Steps 4–12 on pp.106–110.

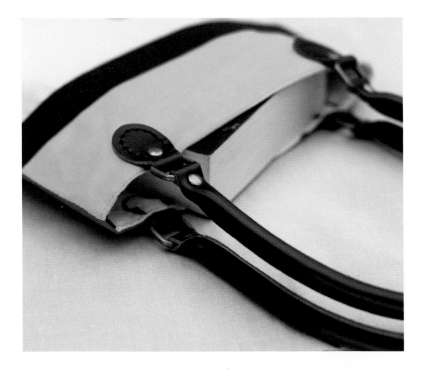

How to **Make a Bias Strip**

A bias strip is a length of fabric that is cut on the bias, or cross (see p.22). This gives it some stretch, which makes it perfect for edging and neatening a curve. You can buy bias binding ready-made, but it's useful to know how to make your own as you can then make it to match your fabric exactly if you need to.

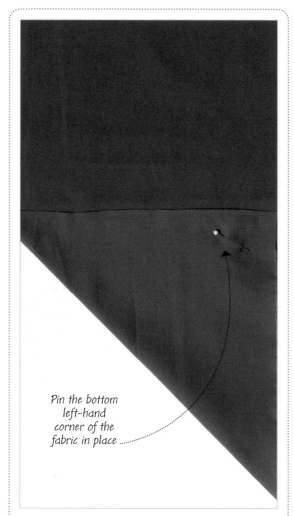

Pin the bottom left–hand corner of the fabric in place ......

Space the chalk lines at the width you want your bias binding ......

1 Place the fabric so the selvedges (see p.22) are on the right and left and the cut edges at the top and bottom. Fold the bottom left-hand corner of the fabric upwards and onto itself at a 45-degree angle. The left-hand selvedge will form a right-angled crease.

2 With the fold pinned in place, use tailor's chalk and a ruler to carefully mark a series of lines parallel with the fold to designate the width of your strips – bias binding is commonly 4cm (1½in) wide. Cut along these lines to make several bias strips of the same width.

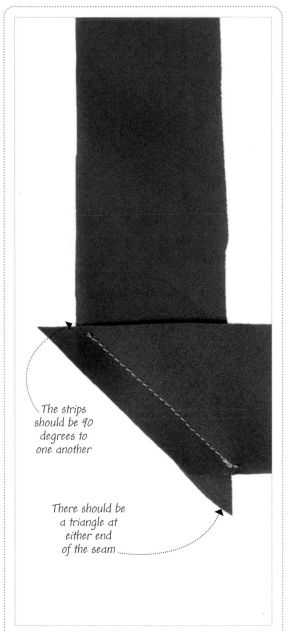

The strips should be 90 degrees to one another

There should be a triangle at either end of the seam

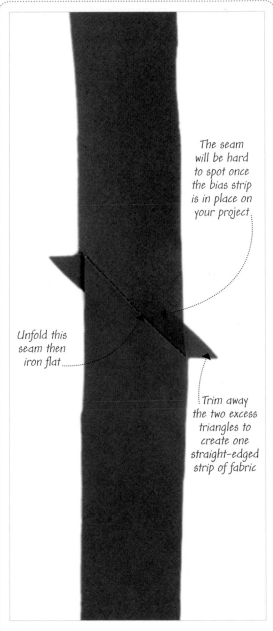

The seam will be hard to spot once the bias strip is in place on your project

Unfold this seam then iron flat

Trim away the two excess triangles to create one straight-edged strip of fabric

3 Place two of the strips right side to right side at 90 degrees to each other so that their angled edges line up. Join the strips together with a line of straight machine stitching. You should end up with a little triangle of overhanging fabric at either end of the seam.

4 Flip the "arm" of the strip over so you have a single straight strip with a diagonal seam running through it. Iron the seam open so that the strip lies completely flat. Trim away the triangles at the seam. Continue to sew strips together until you have the length you need.

Make Bunting

A line of bunting flapping gently in the breeze conjures up sun-filled images of summer parties for all ages and occasions. Make our simple bunting in fabrics of your choice to personalize your party and make it an event your guests will remember long after it's over.

You will need:

Template from p.179 • Fabric: floral or polka dot cotton • Fabric scissors • Pins • Sewing machine Thread • Knitting needle • Iron and ironing board • Bias binding • Buttons

1 Fold the fabric in half, making sure that you fold one selvedge up to meet the other (see p.26) so that the pattern – if your fabric has one – aligns perfectly. Trace the template, cut it out, and pin it onto the fabric through both layers. Cut the triangles out using fabric scissors. Repeat until you have enough triangles.

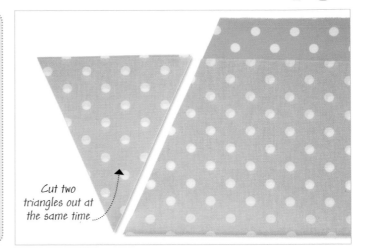

Cut two triangles out at the same time

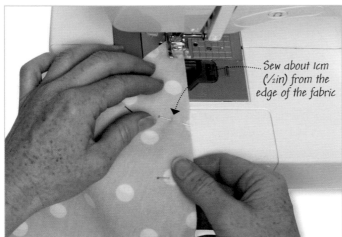

Sew about 1cm (½in) from the edge of the fabric

2 Pin two triangles together, right sides facing, along the two diagonal sides. Beginning at the top of the triangles, machine stitch down towards the point about 1cm (½in) from the edge of the fabric. When you reach the point, lower the needle into the fabric, raise the presser foot, and turn the fabric so the foot is facing along the adjacent side. Lower the foot and continue stitching along the second side.

3 Once you have secured your thread, trim away any excess fabric at the point of the triangle using fabric scissors. Repeat for all of your pairs of triangles.

Remember Trimming away the excess fabric means that when you turn the triangle inside out, it will form a neat point.

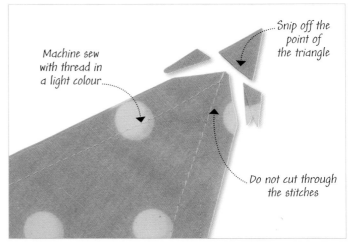

Machine sew with thread in a light colour

Snip off the point of the triangle

Do not cut through the stitches

4 Turn the triangles the right way out and use a knitting needle or similar pointed item to gently push out the points.

Careful! Only push gently, as you don't want to burst through the stitches.

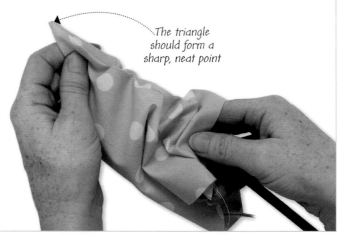

..The triangle should form a sharp, neat point

Start at the point and iron downwards ...

5 Iron all the triangles flat. Ensure that when you iron them you don't allow the fabric to twist from the point – the seams should run very precisely down the sides of the triangle.

6 If you need to, trim along the top of the triangle to make it level, ready for attaching the bias binding or ribbon. Fold bias binding or ribbon over the top edge of the triangle. Ensure that the triangle is pushed right into the fold, then pin in place.

Tip Space the triangles evenly along the bias binding. In this project the triangles were spaced 1cm (½in) apart.

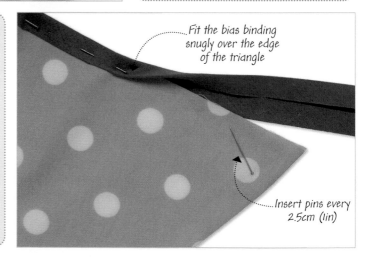

....Fit the bias binding snugly over the edge of the triangle

....Insert pins every 2.5cm (1in)

7 Machine stitch along the edge of the bias binding. Use a straight stitch and choose a thread in a matching colour.

Tip If you position the pins so that they point towards the sewing machine, you will easily be able to pull them out as you go.

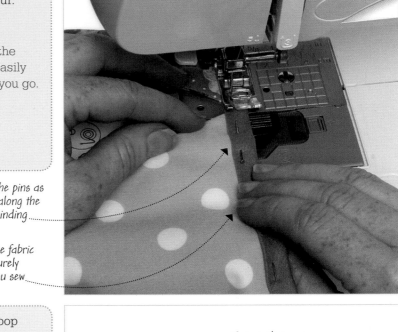

Remove the pins as you sew along the bias binding

Hold the fabric securely as you sew

8 You'll need to create a loop at each end of the bias binding so that you can hang it up. Fold over the end of the bias binding to create a loop of about 2.5cm (1in). Tuck the raw end under and stitch it in place.

Tip For a decorative touch, stitch a pretty button over the folded end of the bias binding.

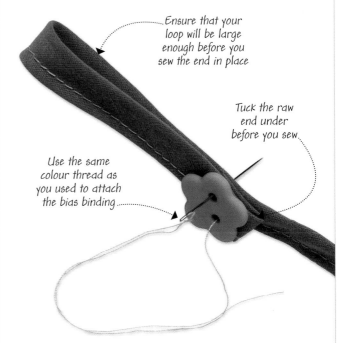

Ensure that your loop will be large enough before you sew the end in place

Tuck the raw end under before you sew

Use the same colour thread as you used to attach the bias binding

The perfect **Bunting**

Beautiful, vintage-style bunting can add the finishing touch to a party. Ensure that your triangles are perfectly pointed and evenly spaced for a professional finish.

Spacing should be equal between the triangles

The triangles should be securely held by the bias binding

The triangles should end in sharp, neat points

Evenly spaced shapes

The triangles should all be equidistant from each other along the bias binding. It doesn't matter what the spacing is – feel free to experiment – but once you have decided, use a tape measure to pin the triangles in the right place.

Securely attached triangles

Your triangles should be firmly sandwiched between the two edges of the bias binding and secure enough that they cannot come loose, even if used outdoors.

Sharp points

The triangles should come to neat, sharp points. Push them out carefully when you turn them inside out and make sure that you iron them flat. When you sew the front and back together, make sure that the two layers of fabric sit completely square on top of each other. If the triangles slip even a little out of place it will be very visible.

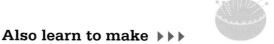

Also learn to make ▶ ▶ ▶

Alternative Shapes

If you've tried your hand at traditional bunting and want to experiment with some different shapes, why not make some from brightly coloured felt to hang in a nursery or child's bedroom? You could link stars, hearts, or flower shapes, or even make letters that spell out a name.

CREATING YOUR BUNTING

If you are making irregular shapes, use felt, as it is a stiff fabric and will hold its shape well without sagging. There are a lot of different colours to choose from, including some that are glittery, so consider using these to add a bit of shimmer to your bunting. Cut out your shapes and edge them with blanket stitch using brightly coloured embroidery thread (see p.57).

Decorate your shapes with puffs (see p.54), ribbons, buttons, or embroidery – whatever takes your fancy. You can link the shapes at the bottom so they don't flap around – unlike traditional

bunting, which should flap around! Do this with a length of narrow ribbon, as in the train bunting below. Lay out the ribbon and position the shapes on top of it so they are evenly spaced. Secure the ribbon to the back of each shape with a few small hand stitches, ensuring that the ribbon is held taut. Finish by linking the shapes at the top with decorative ribbon, using the same technique.

Alternatively, you can attach the shapes to bias binding using the same method as for traditional bunting – just ensure that enough of the shape is sandwiched inside the bias strip to hold it firm.

How to **Upcycle Clothing**

Many people nowadays have taken upcycling, or re-purposing, clothing and other fabric to their hearts. Quite simply, instead of chucking old items out, you find a new use for them. You could transform an old jumper into a cushion cover, use a teeshirt to make a bag (see opposite, below), or even turn an old pillowcase into a child's dress (see pp.124–129).

Wanting to save the planet is one reason why you might do some upcycling. Other reasons are that you can't bear to throw away the much-loved dress that you no longer fit into, that worn-out-in-places jacket that holds happy memories, or the pillowcase whose matching duvet cover has long since vanished. And if those reasons aren't enough, being thrifty is another.

What works?

So what sort of item lends itself to upcycling? The answer is, almost anything – from coats, dresses, and skirts, through trousers, jumpers, ties, and jackets to teatowels, tablecloths, curtains, sheets, and pillowcases. The only limits are your creative and technical skills. For your first upcycling projects, it's best to choose fabrics that are easy to work with, such as cotton, linen, wool, and mixes made from these. As with any other sewing project, avoid very fine, very thick, very stretchy, and very slippery fabrics, especially if you are a beginner sewer. Experiment with charity shop buys before you sew any treasured fabrics.

Making use of what's already there

As you get into upcycling, you'll see how easy it can be to incorporate the elements of an old item – such as pockets, an elasticated waistband, a seam, a neckline, or some buttons – into your upcycled project. Jeans pockets could become apron pockets, an elasticated waistband could be stitched together to make a neck opening for a tunic top, a seam could become the bottom of a bag, while a neckline becomes its opening.

Sources of upcycling material

Once you've been hit by the upcycling bug, you'll find yourself looking at the clothes in your wardrobe, at your household linens, and at the clothes in charity shops and car boot sales in a new light. Everything and anything that's pre-loved can enjoy a second use – right down to its buttons. If you can't incorporate the buttons from a garment in your new project, don't throw them away. It probably won't be long before you can use them to decorate an upcycled bag or hat. And if your own wardrobe and the charity shops weren't enough, the oddments bin in your local fabric shop will start to exert a strange fascination. If the oddments are too small to make a garment, they'll surely be big enough to make an appliqué motif, a pair of apron ties, some dainty drawstring bags, a length of bias tape to trim the armholes and hem of a blouse, or a bunch of fabric puffs you can join together to make a throw.

Upcycling Ideas

Part of the fun of upcycling is seeing the possibilities in items that you normally wouldn't think twice about giving to the charity shop or leaving on the sale rail. Here are a few ideas to get your creative juices flowing.

If your child has grown out of an old, much-loved dress, sew up the bottom and transform it into a peg bag that you can hang on the washing line (see right, above).

Instead of shortening an old skirt to a more fashionable length, why not turn it into an apron or a child's skirt?

When your boyfriend cardigan has finally seen better days, transform it into a cosy pillow or a decorative ruffled bib for a tank top.

If your wardobe is full to bursting with colourful printed teeshirts and you finally realise there just aren't enough days in the year to wear them all, cut them up, stitch them together again and you'll have a unique jersey shift dress. Alternatively, sew up the bottom of one, snip off the sleeves, and transform it into a useful bag (see right, below). Personalize with handmade flowers (see pp.60–63).

When your local upholstery shop is throwing out its old swatch books, gather them up, stitch fabric swatches of the same weight together and make yourself a patchwork dress or jacket.

If you see a bargain dress in the sales in a fabric you adore but that's two sizes too big and a weird shape to boot, use one of your own dresses as a template to cut the dress down to size, remove any sleeves, and use the excess fabric to make a glamorous ruffle at the shoulder.

Has an old shirt finally lost its appeal? Are the collar and cuffs too worn to be respectable? Cut up the back and fronts and use the fabric to line a tote bag or a makeup purse.

Rather than rejecting a charity-shop dress because although you love the fabric, you'd never wear that style, cut it into strips and turn them into a bow-tie turban and matching belt or clutch bag.

Peg Dress Bag

Teeshirt Bag

Upcycle a Pillowcase Dress

If you have a couple of spare pillowcases that are in good condition, why not upcycle them to make this sweet, summery dress? Adapt the style to suit your child's taste – you could substitute the straps for ribbons or customize it using some felt flowers in a matching colour.

You will need:
Fabric: two pillowcases of the same size, one plain, one patterned; two straps, 95 x 4cm (38 x 1½in)
"J" Template from p.180 • Pins • Tape measure • Fabric scissors • Sewing machine • Thread
Bias binding: about 62cm (25in) • Iron and ironing board • Needle • Safety pin

1 First make the straps. With the fabric face down, fold it lengthways in half and crease a line down the centre. Fold the edges inwards to meet the crease, iron in place, then press the folded edges inwards again. Pin then machine sew along the open edge.

Tip You can make ribbon straps if you prefer but you'll need to put a few small stitches in at the arm holes so the ribbon can't slip out.

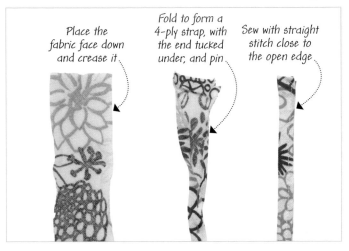

Place the fabric face down and crease it

Fold to form a 4-ply strap, with the end tucked under, and pin

Sew with straight stitch close to the open edge

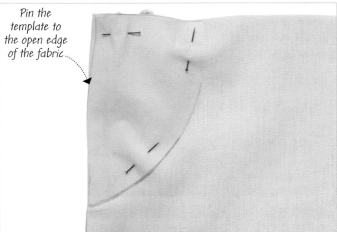

Pin the template to the open edge of the fabric

2 The plain pillowcase forms the main part of the dress. Fold it in half lengthways then cut along the closed short end to remove about 5mm (¼in). You will now have a tube that is open at both ends. Leave it folded. Cut out template "J" on p.180 and pin it to the unfolded edge of the pillowcase in the top corner. Cut around the template to create the arm holes.

3 Decide how long you want the main part of the dress to be, bearing in mind that you will be adding a band of patterned fabric around the bottom and straps to the top. Using a tape measure, measure and mark this length then cut the excess fabric from the bottom. Decide how long you want the patterned band to be then follow Steps 2–3 to cut the patterned pillowcase to form a tube of the correct length.

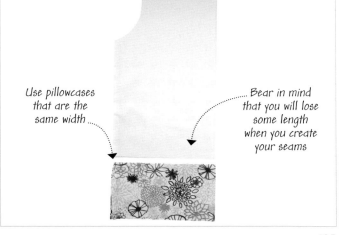

Use pillowcases that are the same width

Bear in mind that you will lose some length when you create your seams

4 Turn the patterned band inside out then slide it onto the bottom of the plain pillowcase so that the edges line up. What will be the top of the patterned band is now lined up with the bottom of the dress. If the pillowcases are the same size they should match up perfectly with their side seams aligned.

Your plain pillowcase should be the right way out

Point the pins downwards to make them easy to sew over

Make sure the edges are flush before you pin

5 Pin the two pieces together, starting at the side seams and working inwards. This will help to keep the two existing pillowcase seams aligned, and to prevent the fabric gaping apart.

Tip Insert the pins every 5cm (2in) to make sure the patterned band is securely attached.

6 Stitch through both layers of fabric using a straight stitch about 1.5cm (½in) from the edge. Remove all the pins. To neaten the raw edge and prevent it from fraying, use a zigzag or overedge stitch (see p.78), or an overlocker (see p.20).

You'll need an overedge foot when using overedge stitch

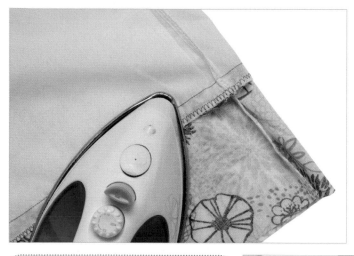

7 Turn the dress inside out, fold the seam towards the bottom, and iron it flat. Turn the pillowcase dress the right way out and iron again.

Tip If one of your fabrics is much darker than the other, make sure that you iron the light fabric over the dark fabric, and not the other way around, or the dark fabric will show through.

8 Measure the bias binding carefully to make sure it matches the length of the arm holes and then cut two lengths to fit. Open out one folded edge of the bias binding and pin it round the arm hole, right side to right side, aligning the raw edge of the binding with the edge of the arm hole. Machine stitch the binding to the arm hole, sewing along the crease in the binding with a straight stitch.

This is the outside of the dress

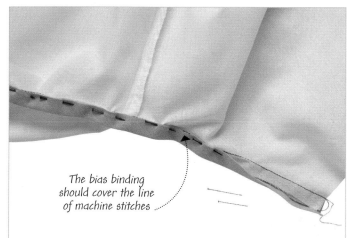

The bias binding should cover the line of machine stitches

9 Fold the bias binding to the inside of the arm hole, pull it gently so it covers the machine stitching, then pin it in place. Space the pins closely to hold the bias binding securely.

Tip If you would like the edges of the arm holes to match the patterned band, use strips of bias binding made from the remnants of the patterned pillowcase (see p.114–115).

10 Use slip stitch (see p.37) to secure the edge of the bias binding on the inside. Remove the pins as you sew but keep the fabric held tight between your fingers.

Remember Use a matching thread colour – green was used here to illustrate the technique.

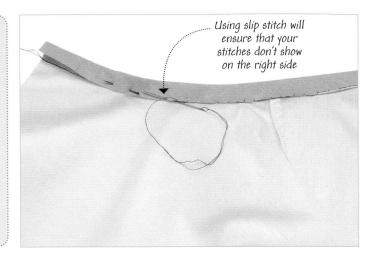

Using slip stitch will ensure that your stitches don't show on the right side

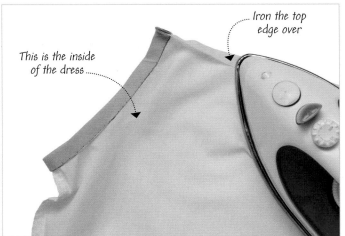

This is the inside of the dress......

..... Iron the top edge over

11 The dress should still be inside out. Turn the top over by 5mm (¼in) and iron it flat. Turn it over again by 2.5cm (1in), and iron, to create a channel for the straps to run through. Machine stitch along the bottom edge of this turnover. Repeat this on the back of the dress.

Tip If you want wider straps than the ones used here, make this channel deeper to fit them through.

12 Attach a safety pin to the end of each strap and thread one through the front channel and one through the back channel. Pull the straps to make gathers and tie the ends together with a bow (see opposite). Make a double-turn hem at the bottom of the dress (see p.92): fold up the bottom edge twice to achieve the desired length, pin in place, then machine the hem close to the upper fold. Remove the pins.

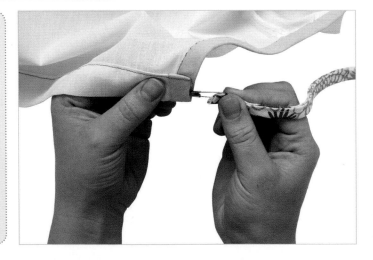

The perfect **Pillowcase Dress**

This dress is simple to make and allows you to transform a few old pillowcases into something new and beautiful. Keep your stitching neat, and tie the straps securely.

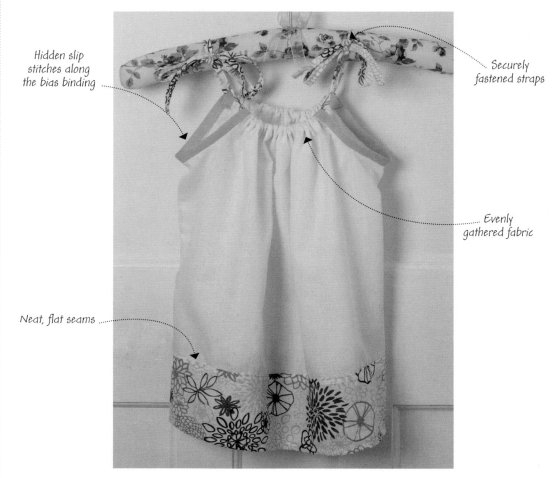

Hidden slip stitches along the bias binding

Securely fastened straps

Evenly gathered fabric

Neat, flat seams

Secure straps

If you make your straps from cotton pillowcase fabric they should hold well when tied into a bow. If, however, you find that they keep coming loose, tie them at the length you want, then put a few stitches through the bow to prevent it from coming undone. If you have chosen to use ribbons, also put a stitch through at the place where the ribbon exits the channel, once you have gathered the fabric. This will ensure that the straps stay in the correct position.

Tidy stitching

With so much of your stitching out on display in this project, it is vital to get it as neat as you possibly can, and to choose threads that closely match your fabrics so that they are well hidden. The dress will need to be able to withstand a fair amount of wear and tear, as well as regular washing, so ensure that your seams are securely neatened, and that you carefully tie off all your threads as you go to prevent any seams coming undone.

3

Take It Further

Stay the course and now you can master simple patchwork, adding a zip, making a "kangaroo" pocket, neatening an edge with a bias strip and making an elasticated waistband. These more advanced techniques pave the way for making a patchwork blanket or cushion cover, a purse, an apron, a door hanging, and a simple skirt and shorts for a child. End by learning how to do some simple mending and you'll never look back.

In this section learn to make:

Purse with a Zip
pp.138–142

Apron
pp.150–156

Door Hanging
pp.158–162

Child's Skirt
pp.166–170

How to **Make Patchwork Squares**

This simple technique will open up a world of beautiful projects to you, from quilts and bags to cushion covers and clothing. The key thing to remember with patchwork is to iron, iron, iron! It's crucial to keep the seams flat so that the patchwork is smooth. Mix and match patterns, colours, and even textures to create your own unique patchwork.

1 Decide how large you want your squares to be, allowing 2cm (¾in) extra for the seams between the patches. Draw the shape on stiff card and cut it out. Lay it on your fabric and draw round it.

2 Cut your squares out using fabric scissors. The number you need will depend on the size and pattern of your patchwork. Cut out some to start and then cut more as you need them.

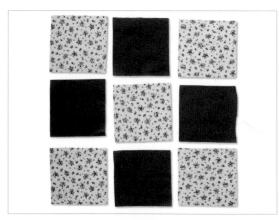

3 Lay out your fabric squares and work out how you want to arrange them. Mix up the patterns and colours for a mismatched look, or alternate the colours and patterns, as shown.

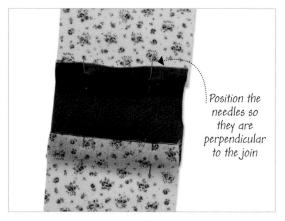

Position the needles so they are perpendicular to the join

4 Pin the patches together in strips of three. Position your pins so that the sewing machine can sew over them easily and you won't have to remove them as you go.

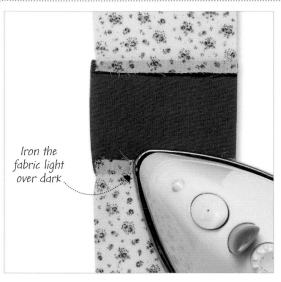

Iron the fabric light over dark

5 Sew along the two seams, 1cm (½in) from the edge. Press the patches with an iron – position the seams so that wherever possible you are ironing the lighter fabric behind the darker fabric.

6 Repeat Steps 4 and 5 twice more so you have three strips of three patchwork pieces. Pin these together to create a three by three square and then machine the seams.

7 Tie off any loose ends, remove all the pins and trim any loose threads or scruffy edges. Iron the patchwork face down to get the seams as flat as possible.

8 Flip the patchwork over and iron it again. You can use this technique to create a patchwork of any size. It is ideal for making cushion covers and quilts (see pp.134–135).

Patchwork Cushion and Quilt

If you mastered how to make patchwork and are looking for some exciting projects so that you can put your new skills into action, why not make a patchwork cushion or blanket? These gorgeous items are easy to make and will add a warm touch to your lounge or bedroom. Use vintage flower prints in soft pastel shades for a designer look.

CREATING YOUR CUSHION

This cushion is incredibly easy to make – all you need to do is sew nine patchwork squares together for each side of the cushion; the patchwork squares used for the example shown are 13 x 13cm (5 x 5in). Lay the sewn-up pieces on top of each other, right sides together, and then sew around three of the edges leaving a 10-cm (4-in) gap in the fourth. Gently turn the cushion inside out through this gap, making sure that you poke out all the corners neatly. Stuff the cusion with wadding until you are happy that it is plump enough, and then sew up the gap using slip stitch (see p.37).

Tip If you want to create a patchwork cushion with a zip, see pp.144–145 to learn how.

CREATING YOUR QUILT

Decide how large you want your quilt to be, and how large your patchwork squares should be for your design. There are no hard and fast rules here – just have a play around with different sizes and colours until you work out a design you like. Here, sixteen large 30-cm (12-in) squares were used to form four rows of four. To add a bit of extra interest and to make the quilt look more professional, narrow strips were added between each row and around the edges. The width of this strip can be as wide or narrow as you like – the strips in the example opposite are 5cm (2in) wide.

Sew four patchwork squares together, as in Steps 1–4 on p.132, and then repeat this three times to create four strips of four. Iron them flat. Attach a 5-cm (2-in) wide band of fabric along one long edge of three of the four patchwork strips, then sew all the strips together so that the three bands of fabric alternate with the four patchwork strips. To add the border, cut another four lengths of fabric and sew them around the four sides of the quilt.

To give the quilt some weight, pad it with sheet wadding of your chosen thickness. Measure the length and width of the patchwork and cut a piece of backing fabric and a layer of wadding to this size. Place the three layers together so the patchwork and backing fabric are next to each other, right side to right side, and the wadding is on top. Pin around one short side and the two long sides, and pin around the other short side, leaving a gap of 30cm (12in) that you will use to turn the quilt to the right side. Machine sew all the sides 1cm (½in) from the edge. Trim away excess wadding and fabric from the corners, then turn the quilt to the right side through the gap. Push the corners out, press well and use slip stitch to close the gap. If you want a quilted effect, stitch through all the layers along the patchwork seams.

How to **Add a Zip**

Knowing how to add a zip is crucial if you want to progress to making projects such as purses (see pp.138–142), pencil cases, or cushion covers (see pp.144–145). But it isn't complicated. Just ensure that if your fabric has a definite "top" and "bottom" that you are absolutely certain that you have it the right way up before you start to sew.

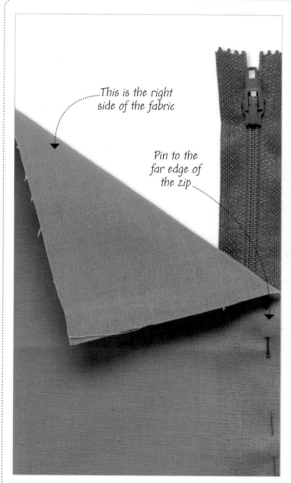

...This is the right side of the fabric

Pin to the far edge of the zip...

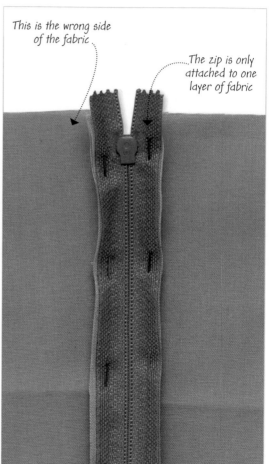

This is the wrong side of the fabric...

The zip is only attached to one layer of fabric

1 Place the right side of the fabric on top of the zip, aligning the edge of the fabric with the far edge of the zip. Pin the fabric in place. Position the pins close to the teeth of the zip. If you are making a purse or pencil case, bear in mind that the edge that you have pinned to the zip will sit at the top.

2 Move the pinned fabric to the right so that it is out of your way, then repeat the process to attach another piece of fabric to the other side of the zip. When you turn the zip and fabric over they will appear as shown above, with your pins visible through the fabric.

Trim the ends,
leaving 5cm (2in)
or so of thread

Iron to form
a sharp fold

Sew visible stitches
along this
line for added
decoration

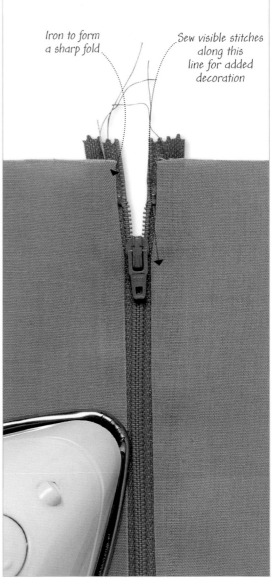

3 Move the fabric out of the way so you can position just one edge of the zip and its attached single thickness of fabric under the foot. Machine stitch from the top of the zip to the bottom, then repeat to sew down the other side of the zip. Trim the ends of the thread.

4 With the zip facing upwards, manipulate the fabric with your fingers so that it sits flat, then iron to make a crisp fold either side of the zip. If you want, you can add a line of stitching on top of these folds – this will help to keep them in place and also makes a decorative feature.

Make a Purse with a Zip

Make this cute little purse from remnants of your favourite fabric to keep your loose change safe in your bag. Or, if you prefer, use the purse to store spare buttons, beads, or safety pins for your sewing projects.

You will need:
Templates from p.180, Leaf A and Leaf B • Fabric: two pieces of patterned outer, two pieces of plain lining, two pieces of fusible interfacing, all 10 x 12.5cm (4 x 5in); felt to decorate • Fabric scissors
Pinking shears • Iron and ironing board • Needle • Embroidery silk • Pins • Zip: 15cm (6in)
Sewing machine • Zip foot • Thread • Elastic and beads

1 Trace the leaf templates given on p.180. Pin them to your felt, and then use pinking shears to cut out the shapes.

Tip Don't feel limited to using leaves as a decoration – you could cut out hearts or stars, or customize the purse with the first letter of your name.

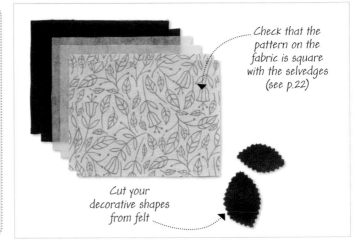

... Check that the pattern on the fabric is square with the selvedges (see p.22)

Cut your decorative shapes from felt ....

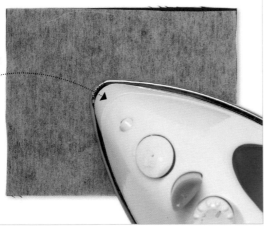

Press the iron firmly to bind the interfacing to the lining ....

2 Iron a piece of fusible interfacing to the wrong side of each piece of lining. Don't move the iron but press firmly in one place. Make sure the interfacing doesn't overhang the lining before you apply your iron.

3 Add your decoration to the piece of fabric that will become the front of the purse. If the pieces are too small to pin, hold them firmly in place as you sew. For embroidery stitches see pp.56–59.

Tip Use three strands of embroidery silk in a contrasting colour to make your stitches stand out against the felt.

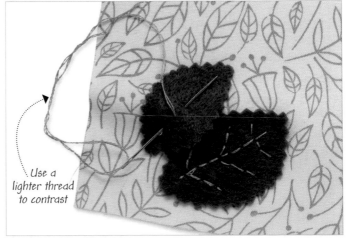

.. Use a lighter thread to contrast

4 Lay one piece of lining onto the table with the interfaced side facing down. Position the zip on top of this so that their edges align, then lay a piece of the outer fabric face down on top. The lining and fabric will be right side to right side with the zip face up between. Pin the three layers together, inserting the pins close to the zip. Repeat to pin the second pieces of lining and fabric to the other side of the zip.

Remember The edge of the fabric that gets pinned to the zip will be the top of your design.

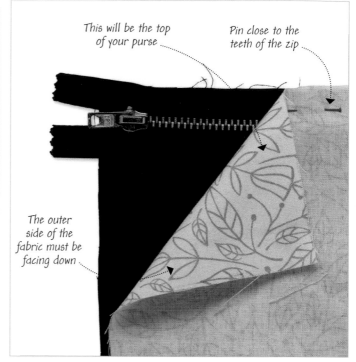

This will be the top of your purse

Pin close to the teeth of the zip

The outer side of the fabric must be facing down

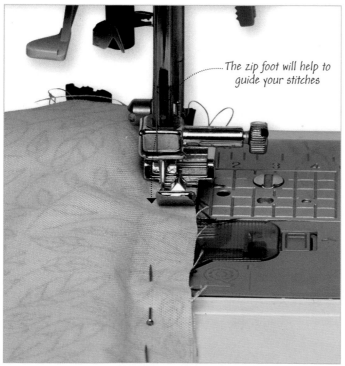

The zip foot will help to guide your stitches

5 Ensure that you have attached a zip foot to your sewing machine. Move the fabric clear so you can position one edge of the zip, one layer of outer fabric, and one piece of interfaced lining under the foot. Carefully sew along one side of the zip, following the line of pins. Use a straight stitch and try to keep the lines as straight as possible. Tie the threads off then turn the purse round and sew along the line of pins on the other side of the zip.

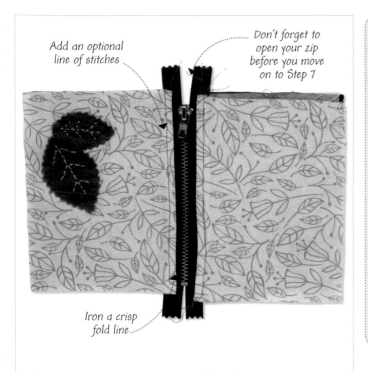

Add an optional
line of stitches

Don't forget to
open your zip
before you move
on to Step 7

Iron a crisp
fold line

6 Open the purse out and place it on the table with the front and back pieces and the zip facing upwards. Iron the fabric firmly so that it sits neatly next to the zip and forms a crisp fold. If you want, machine sew a line of stitches down the sides of the zip to hold the folds in place. Before you move on to Step 7, you must open the zip about three-quarters of the way. This is really important – if you leave it closed you won't be able to turn your purse the right way out in Step 9.

7 Flip the front and back pieces so that their right sides meet and do the same to the lining pieces. Pin the front to the back round the top and two sides but leave a 7-cm (3-in) gap in the lining. You will use this gap to pull the purse through in Step 9.

Tip Space your pins closely to ensure that the layers of fabric stay perfectly aligned as you sew.

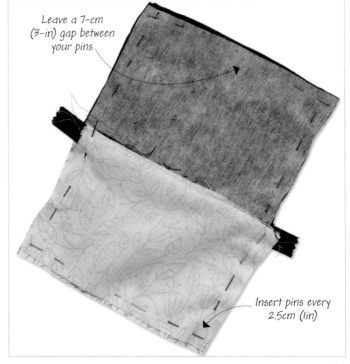

Leave a 7-cm
(3-in) gap between
your pins

Insert pins every
2.5cm (1in)

8 Sew around the edge of the purse leaving the 7-cm (3-in) gap unsewn; stitch about 1cm (½in) from the edge. Cut off any excess fabric at the corners so that they will turn inside out neatly without being bulky, being careful not to cut into your stitches. Trim away any excess zip fabric at either end.

Careful! If you have used a metal zip, be really careful not to sew over it too fast or you could break your needle – go slowly to be on the safe side.

Cut off the excess zip fabric

Trim away the corners

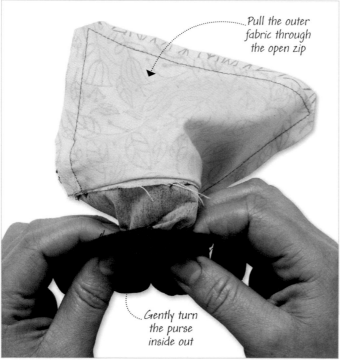

Pull the outer fabric through the open zip

Gently turn the purse inside out

9 Reach through the gap you left in the lining and through the open zip, and gently pull the purse the right way out. Carefully push the corners out so that they are square. Use slip stitch (see p.37) to close up the gap in the lining, with thread in a matching colour. Push the lining into place inside the purse and it is ready to use.

Tip You could use a knitting needle to push the corners out, as long as you are gentle.

The perfect **Purse with a Zip**

This cute purse looks tricky to make, but in fact it's very simple. Get your corners sharp and your stitching straight for a really professional finish.

Neat, right-angled corners

Straight stitching along the zip

A handy elastic zip pull

Easy zipping
You may wish to add a handle to the zip to make it easier to use, especially if the purse is for a child. To create a handle like this, simply thread a piece of elastic through the zipper, add some decorative beads, and then knot the end. Alternatively, you could use a knotted length of ribbon with beads threaded onto it.

Straight patterns
If you are using a patterned fabric with stripes or lines of shapes, take special care to ensure

that when you cut the fabric, you cut in line with the selvedges (see p.22), otherwise the pattern will not be square with the zip, and the whole purse will look wonky.

Secure zip
The zip should feel secure and should open and close easily. Make sure that you have trimmed off any excess at either end before you turn the bag right side out. If you don't, the fabric ends of the zip might show through or affect the shape of your purse.

Also learn to make ▶ ▶ ▶

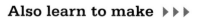

Pencil Case and Cushion Cover

Once you've mastered the technique of inserting a zip, there are any number of different items you can make that use exactly the same method. This lovely pencil case is made from black and white fabric that can be coloured in with fabric pens. Or why not choose a graphic printed fabric for a cushion cover and appliqué some birds and leaves on top?

CREATING YOUR PENCIL CASE

Choose fabrics that are hardwearing, such as thick cotton or canvas, and use a brightly coloured lining. Make the case using the method given on pp.138–142 – the only difference is the dimensions. This case uses fabric that is 24 x 16cm (10 x 6in). For a colour-in case, choose a monochrome, line-drawn print and invest in some fabric pens.

Tip Make sure that the case is long enough to hold your pens or pencils – the average pencil is about 20cm (8in) long.

CREATING YOUR CUSHION COVER

The advantage of creating a cover with a zip is that it can be removed and washed – so don't stuff the cushion with wadding, use a cushion pad instead. Choose a hardwearing fabric with a graphic monochrome print and cut it 2.5cm (1in) larger than the length and width of your pad. Trace the shapes from the monochrome fabric then cut them out of floral fabric. Pin them in place on the cushion front then machine sew around the edges with zigzag stitch. Make the cushion using the method on pp.138–142, but without the lining.

How to **Make a Kangaroo Pocket**

This type of pocket is a variation on a patch pocket, see pp.104–105, and is made and attached in the same way. It is a large pocket that is often found on aprons, sports clothes, and children's dresses.

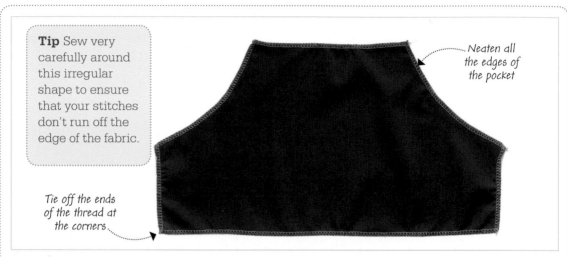

Tip Sew very carefully around this irregular shape to ensure that your stitches don't run off the edge of the fabric.

Neaten all the edges of the pocket

Tie off the ends of the thread at the corners

1 Cut out your pocket to the correct size for your project, remembering that you will lose about 1cm (½in) from each edge when you turn them under. Neaten all the edges with a zigzag or overlock stitch (see p.78 and p.20) to prevent them from fraying and creating a hole in the seam. Secure the ends of the thread carefully (see p.74).

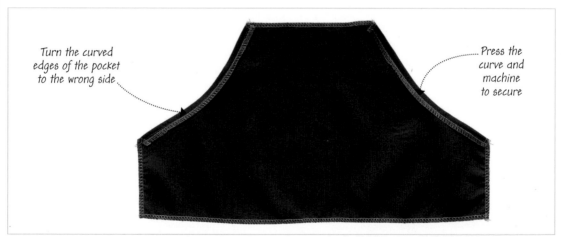

Turn the curved edges of the pocket to the wrong side

Press the curve and machine to secure

2 The curved edges of the pocket will form the pocket opening after it is attached. Evenly turn these curved edges over to the wrong side – manipulate the fabric using your fingers if you need to – and iron the curve flat. Then, using a straight stitch with a matching thread colour, machine the turned, curved edges to secure.

3 Turn all the remaining edges of the pocket over by about 1cm (½in), so that they sit on the wrong side. If the fabric is bulky, trim the corners, then iron the edges in place.

4 Place the pocket on the garment, wrong side of the pocket to the right side of the garment. Make sure the pocket is flat, centred, and straight. Pin the pocket in place.

5 Machine sew the upper edge of the pocket, then down one short straight side, pivot at the corner (see p.79), stitch along the bottom, pivot again, then stitch up the other side.

6 Reinforce the corners with some diagonal stitches. If required, stitch one or two vertical lines down the centre of the pocket, to divide into two pockets. Iron again.

How to **Apply Bias Binding**

The raw edge of a piece of fabric will require neatening to prevent it from fraying. There are several ways to do this. The edge can simply be finished with a zigzag or overlock stitch or it can be pinked. However, finishing the edge with bias binding makes the project a little more luxurious and can add a designer touch to a garment.

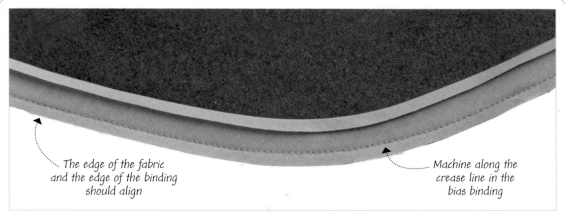

The edge of the fabric and the edge of the binding should align

Machine along the crease line in the bias binding

1 Making your own bias strip is easy (see pp.114–15). Alternatively, you can buy bias binding ready made. Open out one folded edge of the bias binding and pin it along the raw edge of the fabric, right side to right side. Sew the two layers together by stitching along the crease in the binding. Make sure the binding edge aligns with the fabric edge.

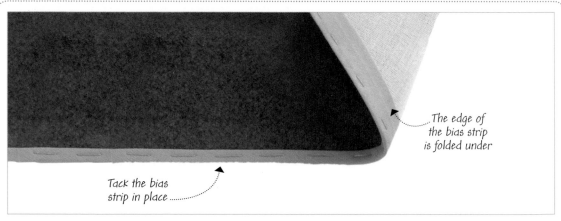

The edge of the bias strip is folded under

Tack the bias strip in place

2 Fold the bias binding over the stitching and under the fabric to the wrong side. The folded edge of the bias strip should remain folded under – it will have a neat appearance on the wrong side. Gently ease the binding in place and pin it along the whole length of the fabric. Use a tacking stitch to hold it in place (see p.36) and remove your pins.

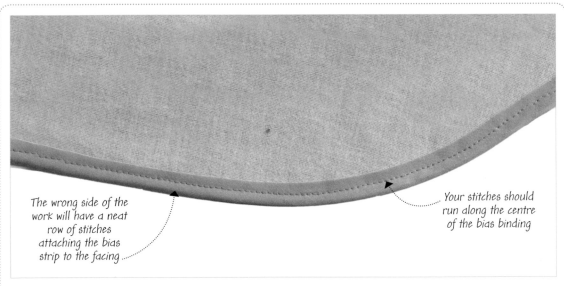

Your stitches should run in the groove between the binding and the fabric

3 With the right side of your fabric facing up, machine stitch along the groove made by the bias-binding-to-fabric stitching. Sew very slowly and carefully around any curves to make sure you don't stray off course. Sew through all the layers. If you don't, the bias strip edge will eventually unfold with wear and tear and washing, and will look ragged.

The wrong side of the work will have a neat row of stitches attaching the bias strip to the facing

Your stitches should run along the centre of the bias binding

4 When you turn your fabric over to the wrong side the bias-bound edge will have a neat finish, with the stitches running along the centre of the binding. As an alternative to machine stitching the second seam you can slip stitch (see p.37) the binding to the back of the fabric using matching thread. No stitches will be visible on the front.

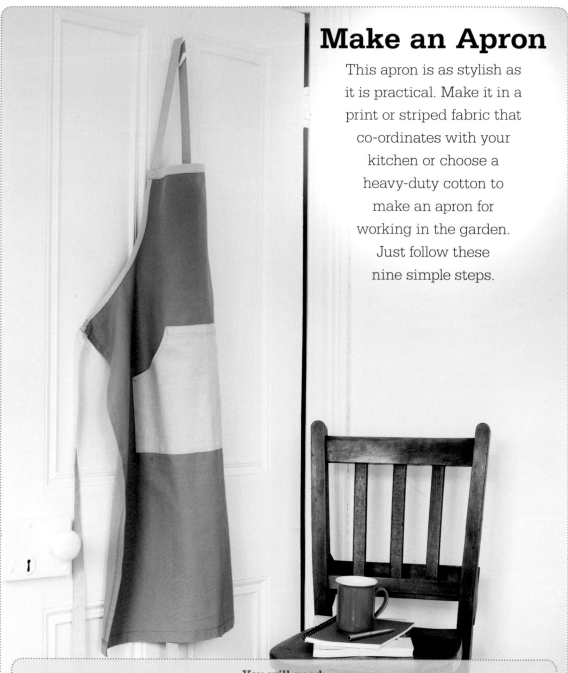

Make an Apron

This apron is as stylish as it is practical. Make it in a print or striped fabric that co-ordinates with your kitchen or choose a heavy-duty cotton to make an apron for working in the garden. Just follow these nine simple steps.

You will need:

Templates from p.184 • Fabric: heavy duty cotton or linen in two contrasting colours – for dimensions see p.184; apron strings fabric, two strips of 90 x 8cm (36 x 3in); neck tie fabric, 60 x 8cm (24 x 3in) • Bias binding, three pieces 50cm (20in) long – buy ready-made or make it yourself Fabric scissors • Sewing machine • Overedge foot • Thread • Pins

1 Cut out your fabric pieces using the templates given on p.184. If you choose to make your own bias binding (see pp.114–115), make it from the same fabric as your kangaroo pocket. Neaten the two straight sides and the bottom of Apron Piece 1, using a zigzag, overedge, or overlock stitch.

Neaten the three sides that won't be edged with bias binding

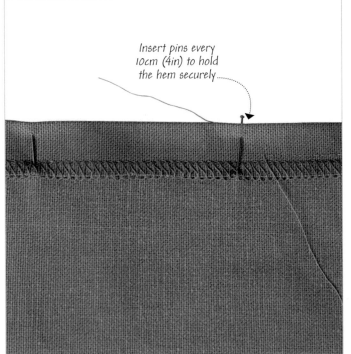

Insert pins every 10cm (4in) to hold the hem securely

2 Turn over the three straight edges that you have just neatened by about 2cm (¾in), folding them to form a hem on the back of the fabric. Iron this hem flat and then pin it in place. Using a straight stitch, machine sew in place. Sew alongside the overlock or overedge stitching.

Tip Place the pins perpendicular to the edge of the fabric so that you can machine sew over them.

3 Pin homemade bias binding in place at the top edge of Apron Piece 1, right side to right side and aligning the edge of the binding with the edge of the apron. If you are using bought bias binding, open up one of the creases and pin the unfolded binding to the edges (see Step 1, p.148). You will sew along this open crease.

Tip Position the pins closely so that the bias strip cannot move.

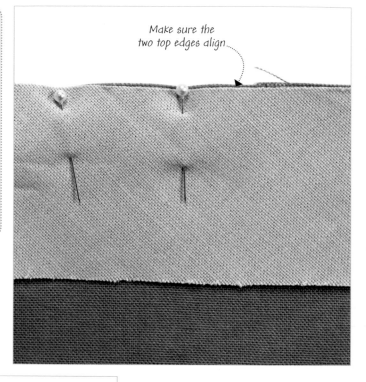

Make sure the two top edges align

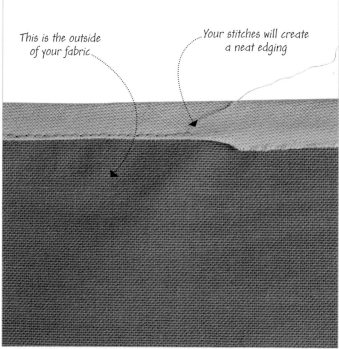

This is the outside of your fabric

Your stitches will create a neat edging

4 Machine sew the bias binding in place. For homemade binding, sew about 1cm (½in) from the edge; for bought binding, sew along the crease. Fold the binding over the stitching and under the fabric to the wrong side. Pull it tight and pin it in place. Tack, then remove the pins (see Step 2, p.148). On the right side, machine along the groove to secure (see Step 3, p.149). Repeat Steps 3 and 4 above to apply binding to the two arm holes.

5 In order to create the two compartments of your pocket, you will need to mark a line that runs down the centre. Use a tape measure to ensure that your line is straight and centred, then mark it using a line of tacking stitches (see p.37).

Tip Use a brightly coloured thread so that your line of tacking stitches stands out.

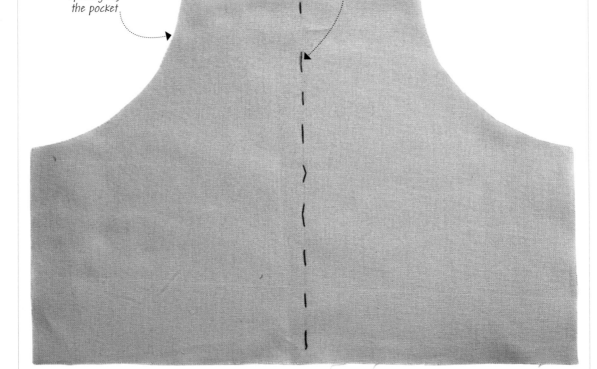

Mark the centre of the pocket.

The curved edges will be the openings of the pocket.

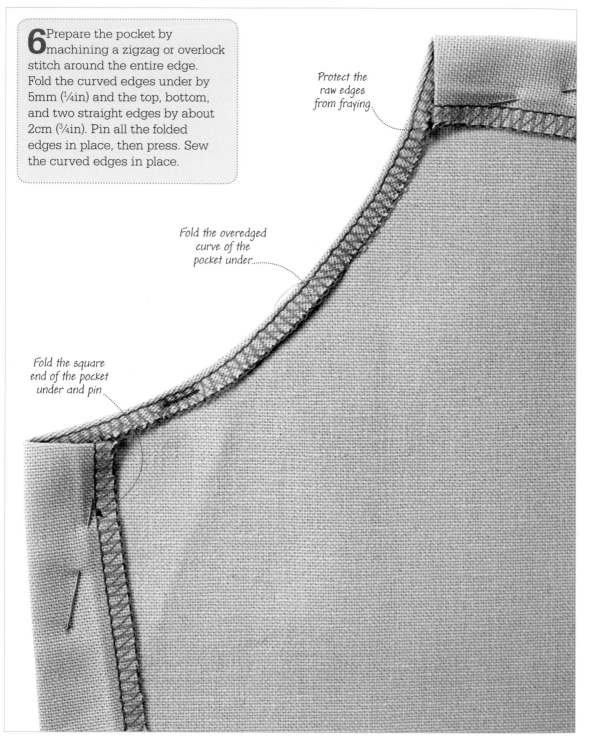

6 Prepare the pocket by machining a zigzag or overlock stitch around the entire edge. Fold the curved edges under by 5mm (¼in) and the top, bottom, and two straight edges by about 2cm (¾in). Pin all the folded edges in place, then press. Sew the curved edges in place.

Protect the raw edges from fraying

Fold the overedged curve of the pocket under

Fold the square end of the pocket under and pin

7 Position the pocket 32cm (13in) from the top edge and centre it horizontally. Pin it in place and sew along the straight edges with a matching thread. Add diagonal stitches to reinforce the corners and sew two rows of stitches down the centre of the pocket. Remove the tacking stitches.

Do not sew up the curved edges – these form the openings of the pockets

Sew a rectangle of stitches on the top edge to reinforce it

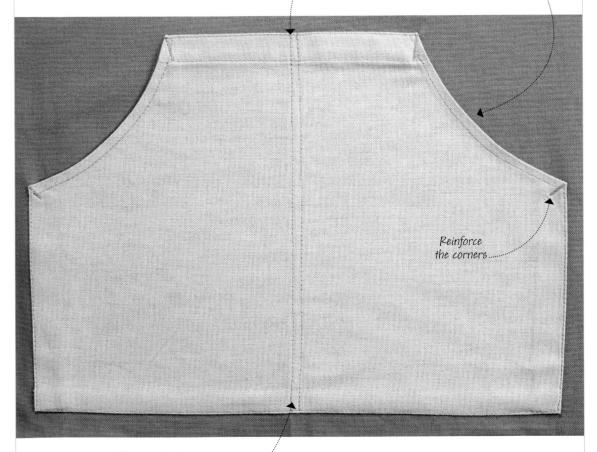

Reinforce the corners

Follow your tacking stitches to create the two halves of your pocket

8 Create the apron strings and the neck tie: fold the fabric strips down the centre, lengthways. Fold the edges in to the centre, then fold each strip in half again so that it is four layers thick. Pin, then machine sew along the open edges (see p.95).

Fold the raw edges inwards

Pin the end under before attaching

9 Attach the two apron strings first by pinning them in place to the back of the apron. Machine sew, creating a rectangle of stitches, then join the four corners with an "X". Attach the neck tie to the corners at the top of the apron using the same technique.

Careful! Ensure that the neck tie isn't twisted before you sew.

Overlap at least 2.5cm (1in) so that the straps are secure

The perfect **Apron**

This simple project requires you to put together lots of the skills you've already learned. Ensure that the ties are securely fastened, and this apron will last you for years.

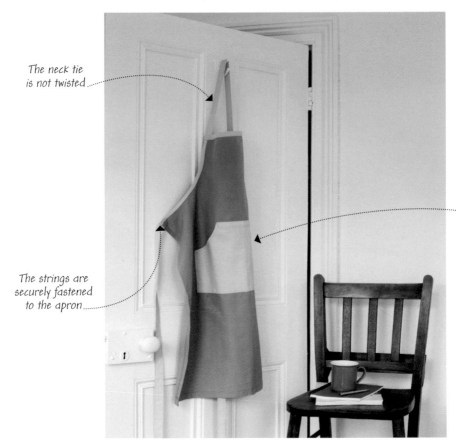

The neck tie is not twisted

The pocket should be straight and centred horizontally

The strings are securely fastened to the apron

Straight pocket

Your pocket should sit exactly in the middle of your apron and must not be wonky. Ensure that you measure it carefully before and after you pin it in place. If you want one large pocket rather than two small compartments, omit the central lines of stitching applied in Step 7.

Secure straps

Make sure that your apron strings will be the right length before you cut the fabric. If you want them longer or shorter, this is the moment to adjust them. If you need to make your neck

tie longer or shorter, adjust this too. Make sure that when you come to sew your straps onto your apron, you overlap the fabrics by about 2.5cm (1in) so that they are securely attached by the stitching.

Adjusting the size

If you want to make an apron for a child using the same pattern, reduce all the measurements by a given percentage. Measure your child to work out how long the apron should be then calculate what fraction of the original measurement this is.

Make a Door Hanging

Bathroom clutter, bedroom clutter – what are you supposed to do with it all? The answer is – store it in a stylish door hanging like this one. Make it from sturdy cotton so it stays firm when fully laden, add a coat hanger and voilà – it's ready to hang from the back of any door!

You will need:
Templates from p.185 • Fabric: heavy duty cotton or linen – for dimensions see p.185
Stretch ribbon: 50cm (20in) • Decorative braid: 1.2m (48in) • Fabric scissors • Sewing machine
Overedge foot • Thread • Pins • Tailor's chalk • Coat hanger

1 Cut out all your fabric pieces using the templates given on p.185. Lay the front piece out in front of you and position the stretch ribbon across it, 10cm (4in) from the top edge. Pin it in place. Machine sew vertical rows of stitches at intervals along it – the spacing will depend on the items you plan to store.

Tip Lay out the items before you sew, to ensure that they will fit.

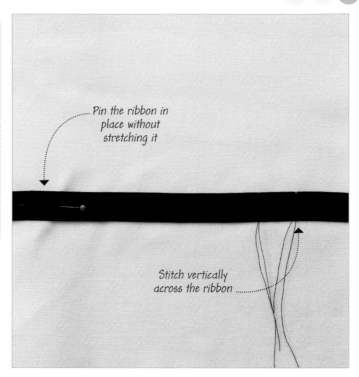

Pin the ribbon in place without stretching it

Stitch vertically across the ribbon

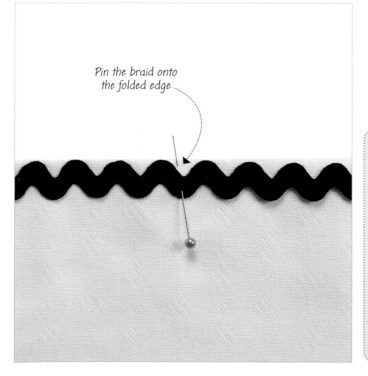

Pin the braid onto the folded edge

2 Fold both pieces of pocket fabric in half, lengthways with the wrong sides of the fabric facing in. Iron them flat. Pin your decorative braid or trimming along the folded edges and then stitch it carefully into place. Remove the pins.

Tip Sew very slowly to ensure that you stitch in a straight line along the centre of the braid. If you don't, the braid will gape.

3 Each of the pockets will have three sections divided by a pleat held in place with a line of stitching. Lightly mark with tailor's chalk on the reverse of each piece of pocket fabric 20cm (8in) and 40cm (16in) from the left-hand edge of the pocket. Gather the fabric into a pleat around each mark, pin it, and iron it so that it forms the shape shown in the picture, left. Line up the raw edge of the lower pocket with the bottom edge of the front piece and pin in place. Machine a vertical line of stitching through the centre of each pleat to hold it in place.

Machine sew the lines that divide up your pockets

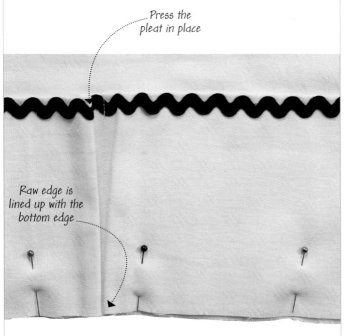

...Press the pleat in place

Raw edge is lined up with the bottom edge ...

4 Iron the pleats into place, manipulating the fabric to make sure that it comes together at the bottom of each pleat, creating sharp "V" shapes. This will cause the upper edge of each pocket section to tip forwards slightly. With your three sections created and your lower edges pinned in position, machine sew the pocket at either end to secure it. You don't need to sew along the bottom edge, as this will be secured when you sew the hanging together in Step 8.

5 Measure 27cm (11in) at intervals from the top edge of the front piece and mark these points with pins. Run a row of tacking stitches along the pins at the 27cm (11in) line in a bright thread colour. This is the line for positioning the upper pocket. With right sides together and the decorated edge of the upper pocket hanging down towards the bottom, pin the raw edge of the pleated pocket along the positioning line. Machine sew in place 1cm (½in) from the edge, then remove the pins.

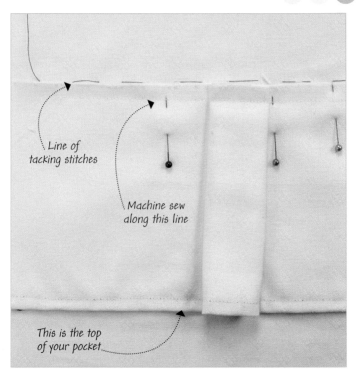

Line of tacking stitches

Machine sew along this line

This is the top of your pocket

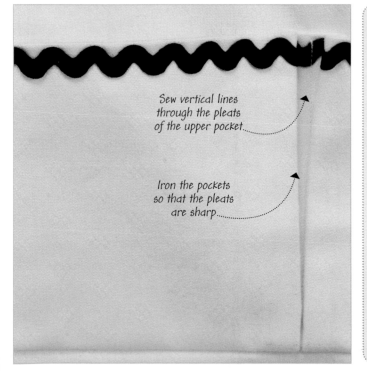

Sew vertical lines through the pleats of the upper pocket

Iron the pockets so that the pleats are sharp

6 If you have ended up with a lot of bulky fabric in the bottom of your pocket, trim this away carefully, taking care not to snip the stitches or any of your fabric. Flip the pocket up into position and machine sew each end to the sides of the front piece. Machine a vertical line of stitches through the centre of each pleat. Iron the pleats in place.

7 Lay the coat hanger on the wrong side of the back piece and draw around it with chalk. Pin the front and back pieces, right side to right side all the way around except for a gap of 20cm (8in) along the bottom edge and a gap of about 1cm (⅜in) at the centre top for the coat hanger. The pockets will now be sandwiched between the front and back.

The front and back are right side to right side

The pins follow the shape of the hanger

The centre of the hanger is marked with chalk

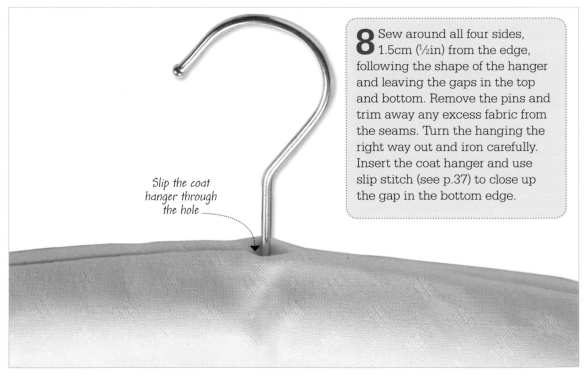

8 Sew around all four sides, 1.5cm (½in) from the edge, following the shape of the hanger and leaving the gaps in the top and bottom. Remove the pins and trim away any excess fabric from the seams. Turn the hanging the right way out and iron carefully. Insert the coat hanger and use slip stitch (see p.37) to close up the gap in the bottom edge.

Slip the coat hanger through the hole

The perfect **Door Hanging**

The trickiest part of this door hanging is the pockets. Make sure that they
are equal widths, with neatly pressed pleats and you can't go wrong!

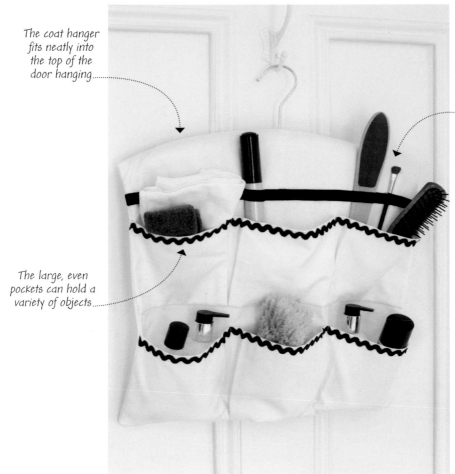

*The coat hanger
fits neatly into
the top of the
door hanging*

*The stretch ribbon
holds tall items
in place*

*The large, even
pockets can hold a
variety of objects*

Even pockets

Your pockets should be of equal width. You
can make as many pockets as you want but
you will need to adapt the length of your pocket
fabric to suit: if you use the same length as in
this project and only make two pockets, there
will be too much slack and the pockets will gape
open. Likewise, if you want a greater number
of pockets, this length of fabric will produce
narrow pockets that won't hold very much.

Securely fastened hanger

Because you drew around it in Step 7, your
coat hanger should fit perfectly into the top of
your door hanging. Make sure that when you
create the channel for the metal hook to slide
through you secure the thread on either side
so that the seams do not begin to unravel
once the weight of the hanging – and any
items you store in it – is placed upon them.

How to **Add an Elastic Waistband**

Elasticated waistbands feature on many items of clothing, from skirts and trousers, to casual jackets and dresses. Knowing how to add an elastic waistband to garments is therefore a very useful skill and one you will use time and time again. The technique below shows you how to make a deep waistband to thread your elastic through.

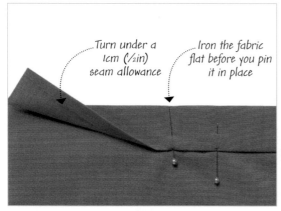

Turn under a 1cm (½in) seam allowance

Iron the fabric flat before you pin it in place

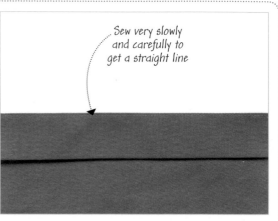

Sew very slowly and carefully to get a straight line

1 Turn over 1cm (½in) and iron it flat. Measure your elastic to work out how deep you need to make your waistband and add 1cm (½in). Turn this over, iron, and then pin in place.

2 Machine stitch a straight line along the top, 2mm (¹⁄₁₆in) from the edge of the fold. This is the top edge of the channel that will enclose the elastic.

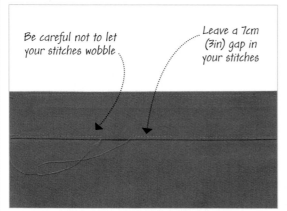

Be careful not to let your stitches wobble

Leave a 7cm (3in) gap in your stitches

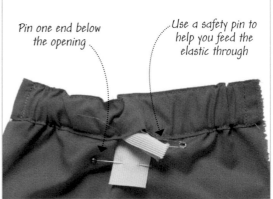

Pin one end below the opening

Use a safety pin to help you feed the elastic through

3 Machine stitch the lower edge of the fold 2mm (¹⁄₁₆in) from the edge to create the bottom of the channel. Leave a gap of about 7cm (3in) so that you can insert the elastic.

4 Cut a piece of elastic long enough to fit round the waist comfortably. Pin one end of the elastic to the fabric. Pin a safety pin to the other end and feed it through the channel.

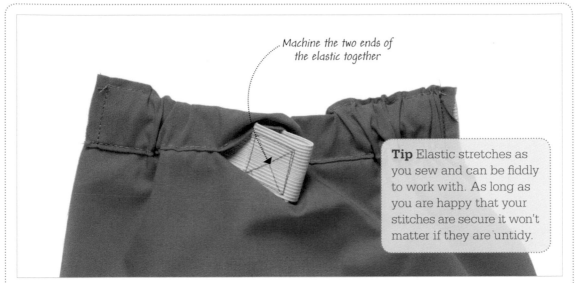

Machine the two ends of
the elastic together

Tip Elastic stretches as you sew and can be fiddly to work with. As long as you are happy that your stitches are secure it won't matter if they are untidy.

5 When you have fed the elastic right the way through the channel, pull the two ends of the elastic together. Pin them securely to each other so that they can't come apart as you sew. Machine stitch a square shape with an "X" across it to join the two ends. This will strengthen the join so it doesn't come apart with everyday wear.

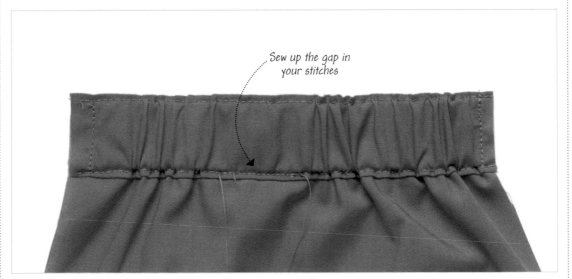

Sew up the gap in
your stitches

6 Push the elastic back into the channel and work it round with your fingers to make sure that the waistband is evenly gathered. Pin the gap closed then stitch it up to enclose the elastic inside the channel. Sew neatly in a matching thread colour so that the stitches will be hard to spot once you are wearing the skirt.

Make a Child's Skirt

Your little girl will simply love this adorable cotton skirt –
and you'll love how easy it is to dress her in it. No fiddly
buttons or zips: just a made-to-measure elasticated
waistband. If you create an extra long hem you will
be able to let the skirt down as she grows.

You will need:
Fabric: the size of the fabric and elastic will depend on the size of your child – see Step 1 for advice
Fabric scissors • Pins • Sewing machine • Overedge foot • Thread
Iron and ironing board • Safety pin • Needle • Decorative ribbon: 110cm (44in)

1 As an approximate guide, for a two- to three-year-old use a piece of fabric 110 x 35cm (44 x 14in); for a three- to four-year-old use 110 x 38cm (44 x 15in). For the length of the elastic: measure your child's waist and add 2.5cm (1in) to that measurement. Once the elastic is in place with the ends sewn together, it will be a comfortable fit. Cut your fabric. Pin the short edges together with the right sides facing in.

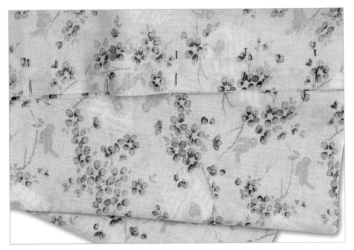

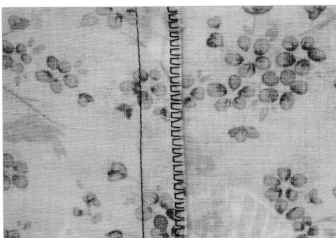

2 Sew along the short edge with a straight machine stitch, leaving a margin of about 1cm (½in). Remove the pins. Neaten the raw edge with an overedge or zigzag stitch (see p.78) to stop it fraying. Iron the seam to one side.

Remember It is important to finish the raw edges or they could fray and cause holes in the seam.

3 If you are using 2cm (¾in) elastic, turn 5cm (2in) of fabric at the waist edge to the wrong side and iron flat. If your elastic is wider than this, make the fold deeper. This fold will create the channel that will hold your elastic, so it is important to get the depth correct.

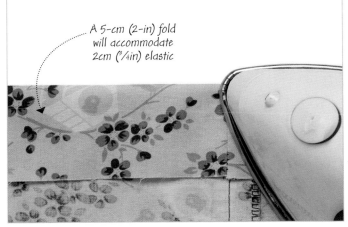

A 5-cm (2-in) fold will accommodate 2cm (¾in) elastic

4 Tuck the raw edge under and iron it in place. Your channel will now be about 2.5cm (1in) deep. Pin it securely, spacing the pins every 7cm (3in) or so. Position them facing outwards so you can easily sew over them and then remove them afterwards.

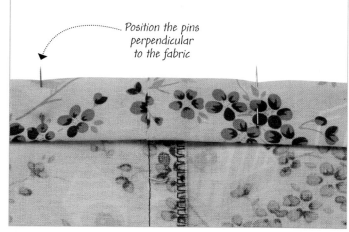

Position the pins perpendicular to the fabric

Stop when you reach your marker pin

The two rows of stitches should be just under 2.5cm (1in) apart

5 Sew around the turnover, a few mm ($\frac{1}{16}$in) from the fold. Tie off the ends of the thread and remove the pins. When sewing along the bottom edge of this turnover you'll need to leave about a 7-cm (3-in) gap in your stitching, so that the elastic can be fed in and pulled through. Use a pin to mark your finishing point. Start stitching about 7cm (3in) beyond this, and then stop when you get back round to the pin.

6 Attach a safety pin to one end of the elastic and feed it through the channel. It may help to pin the other end to the skirt to stop the elastic being pulled right through (see pp.164–165). When the pin emerges from the end of the channel, check that the elastic hasn't twisted, then pin the ends together so they overlap by about 4cm (1½in).

The safety pin helps you pull the elastic through

7 Sew over the overlapped ends to form a rectangle with an "X" across it. This will make the join extra-secure. Remove the pin that holds the ends together as soon as you have sewn the first line of stitches: you won't be able to sew over the pin – the first line of stitches will keep everything in place until you have finished. Secure the thread, then work the elastic through the channel so the waistband is evenly gathered.

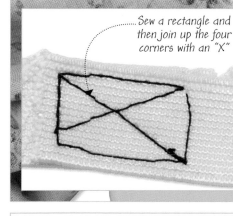

Sew a rectangle and then join up the four corners with an "X"

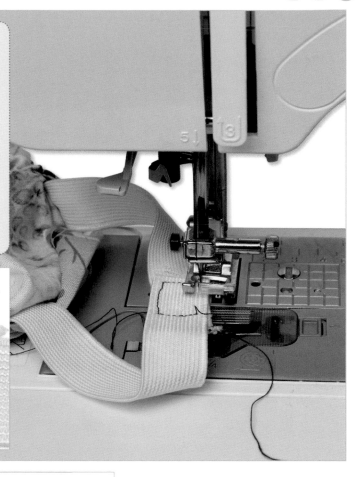

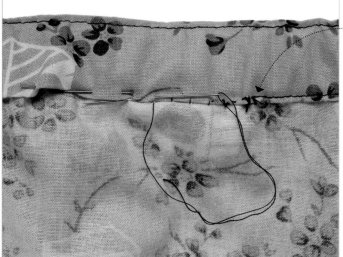

Use the same thread colour as you used in your machine

8 Use slip stitch (see p.37) to sew up the gap, sealing the elastic inside the channel.

Careful! Make sure that you do not catch the elastic in your stitches as you close up the gap. If you do, it will prevent the elastic from stretching.

9 Before you stitch the hem, you'll need to work out how long the skirt should be. Try it on your child and measure the length. Turn the lower edge to the wrong side so the fold is where you want the skirt to end. Here it was turned over by 2.5cm (1in). Iron the fold in place, then tuck the raw edge under, iron again, then pin. Machine carefully along the upper fold using a straight stitch. Remove the pins.

Position the pins so you can easily sew over them

10 Measure round the bottom of the hem and cut your ribbon to this length, plus a little for an overlap. Place one end of the ribbon at the skirt side seam. Pin it round the hemline on top of the stitching, overlapping it slightly at the end. Machine sew in place.

Tip If you feel confident, you can attach the ribbon at the same time as you sew the hem. Pin the ribbon to the right side of the folded hem in Step 9, then sew through the ribbon and the hem together.

Your ribbon trim will cover up your hemline stitches

The perfect **Child's Skirt**

This simple skirt is easy to customize with ribbons or trimming to make it your own. Make sure you have measured carefully to get the perfect fit.

The fabric is gathered evenly along the elastic.

The skirt is the perfect size for your child

The ribbon trim runs parallel to the bottom of the skirt.

The perfect size

Your skirt will be the desired length and size if you have carefully measured throughout the process and taken your seam allowances into account when cutting your fabric. If you want the skirt to last as your child grows, make it from a longer length of fabric than you actually need and turn up a deeper hem at the bottom. This can be unpicked later, when your child grows, let out to lengthen the skirt, and then re-hemmed.

Adapting these techniques

If you've made this skirt and now feel inspired to make garments that are a little more complex, why not start by making the simple shorts on pp.172–173? This lovely project will put into practice many of the techniques that you will have used to make your skirt.

Also learn to make ▶ ▶ ▶

How to **Make Shorts**

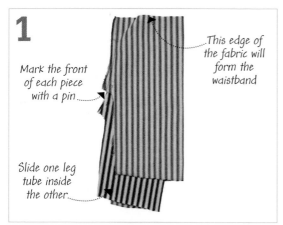

1

Mark the front of each piece with a pin

...This edge of the fabric will form the waistband

Slide one leg tube inside the other

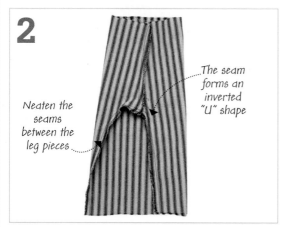

2

Neaten the seams between the leg pieces

The seam forms an inverted "U" shape

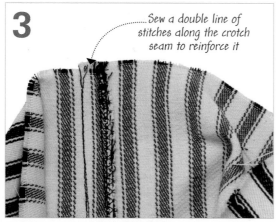

3

...Sew a double line of stitches along the crotch seam to reinforce it

You might look at a pair of shorts and think that they are far beyond your technical reach, but don't be put off. These simple shorts rely on many of the techniques you will have used before, when making a child's skirt (see pp. 166–170), so why not give it a go? If you are feeling creative, you could sew on a decorative fly for a professional finish.

PREPARING THE LEGS

Using the template on p.185, cut out your pieces to the size that you need. Mark the front of each piece using a pin – this will prevent you getting the two pieces round the wrong way. Fold each leg piece in half so that the right sides of the fabric face inwards – pin them to create two leg pieces. On each piece, sew a seam from the waistband down to the crotch, and then overedge it to neaten. You will have created two leg tubes. Turn one leg tube the right way out and then slip it inside the leg that is inside out. Ensure that your two marker pins line up – this is crucial. The crotch joins must align.

STITCHING THE LEGS

Match up the edges that run up and down the inside of the leg pieces and pin them together. Machine sew the pieces together, stitching about 1cm (½in) from the edge of the fabric. Trim away any excess fabric to neaten and then overlock the edges.

FINISHING YOUR SHORTS

Turn the shorts the right way out. Sew two lines of thread along the central seam – this is the seam that runs from the front of the shorts, between the legs and up the back – to reinforce it. Measure your child to work out how long you want your shorts to be, and create the waistband and leg hems as you did for the child's skirt (see pp.166–170).

How to **Darn a Hole and Unpick a Stitch**

It is important to know how to darn holes in knitted garments such as socks or jumpers, because a stitch in time could indeed prevent nine. Another handy technique to have up your sleeve when mending, is knowing how to unpick stitches: many repairs need this technique. Unpick your stitches carefully to avoid damaging the fabric.

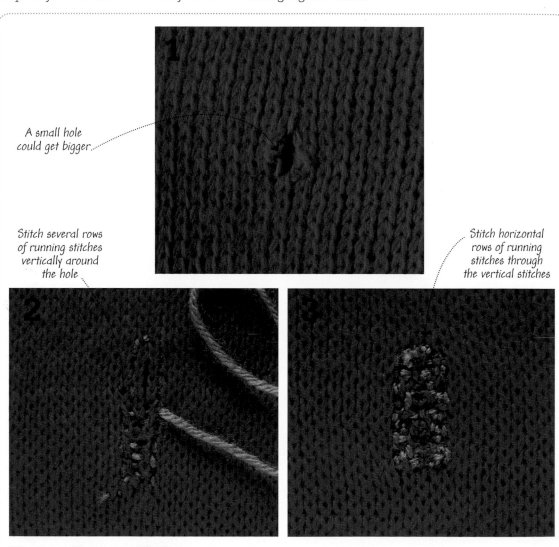

A small hole could get bigger

Stitch several rows of running stitches vertically around the hole

Stitch horizontal rows of running stitches through the vertical stitches

How to **Darn a Hole**

If you find a hole in a jumper or pair of socks, it is always worth darning it while it is still small so that you can stop it from unravelling even further. Simply stitch vertical stitches to strengthen the fabric, then close the hole by stitching horizontally.

Small scissors

This is a simple method for unpicking stitches. Gently pull the two pieces of fabric apart and, using small, sharply pointed scissors, snip through the stitches. Remove all the tiny pieces of cotton before restitching the seam.

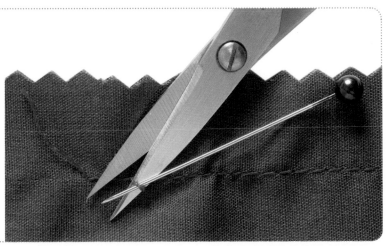

Seam ripper

A seam ripper is a useful tool for removing stitches from seams in light to heavyweight fabrics. Carefully slide its thin, sharp blade under a stitch to cut it through. If you cut through every fourth or fifth stitch, it will encourage the whole seam to unravel.

Pin and scissors

If your stitches are too small for a seam ripper or scissors, use this technique instead. Slide a pin into the stitch and wiggle it around to loosen it. Once it is loose, insert a pair of small, sharp scissors and snip through the thread. Repeat every few stitches.

How to **Mend a Tear**

When a garment gets a tear in it, it might seem as though it is ruined. However, a tear can be very quickly remedied with the help of some fusible mending tape and some new stitching. By applying the fusible mending tape to the wrong side of the fabric, it will be hardly noticeable once you've finished.

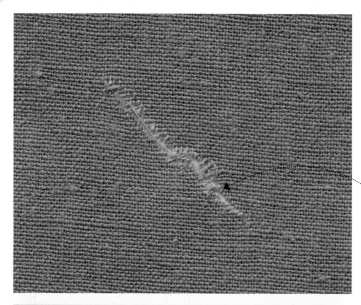

1 Measure the length of the tear in your garment, being careful not to rip it further as you handle it. Cut a piece of fusible mending tape that will fit over the tear, leaving about 1cm (½in) extra on either end.

Measure the length of the tear

2 On the wrong side of the fabric, carefully place the fusible mending tape over the tear, ensuring that the tear is "closed" and not gaping open under the tape. Use an iron to fuse the tape in place (see p.82). Make sure it is securely attached.

Ensure that the mending tape completely covers the tear before you iron

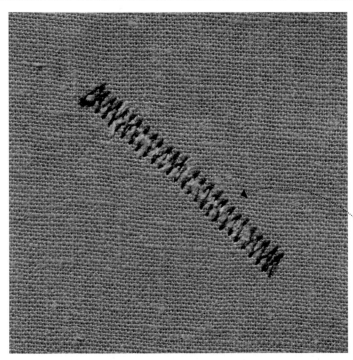

3 Turn the fabric over so that the tear is face up. Using a zigzag machine stitch, carefully sew along the tear line – this will bind the fabric to the mending tape so that the hole cannot reopen. Use a matching thread colour so that the join is as invisible as possible.

Use a closely worked, narrow zigzag stitch

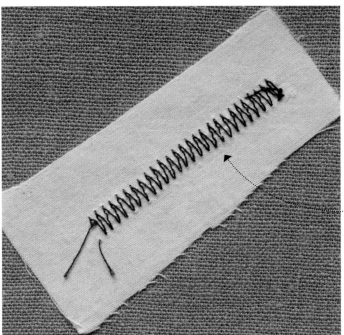

4 Turn your fabric over and carefully trim away any excess mending tape from around the line of stitches. Take care not to snip too close to the stitches or through the fabric. Your tear is now mended.

On the wrong side, the zigzag stitching will be visible on top of the fusible tape

Useful Templates

Use these templates to ensure that your all project pieces are the correct size. The shapes on pp.178–183 are given at the correct size and can be traced from the book as they are; the templates on pp.184–185 will need enlarging to the correct size. Follow the instructions given.

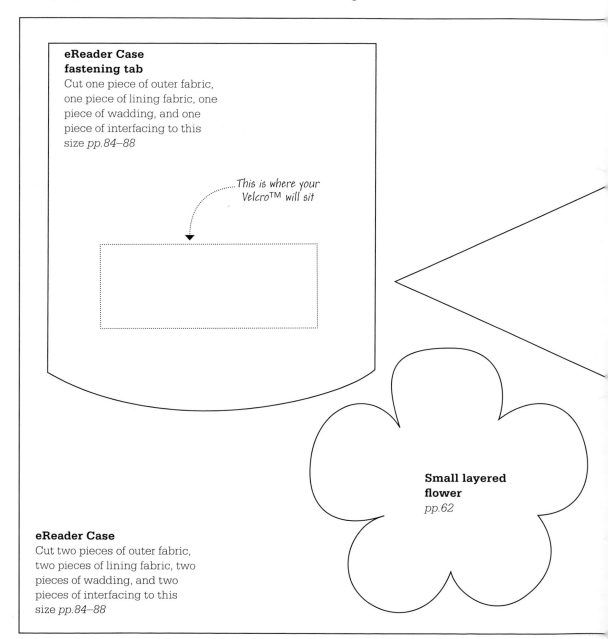

eReader Case fastening tab
Cut one piece of outer fabric, one piece of lining fabric, one piece of wadding, and one piece of interfacing to this size *pp.84–88*

...*This is where your Velcro™ will sit*

Small layered flower
pp.62

eReader Case
Cut two pieces of outer fabric, two pieces of lining fabric, two pieces of wadding, and two pieces of interfacing to this size *pp.84–88*

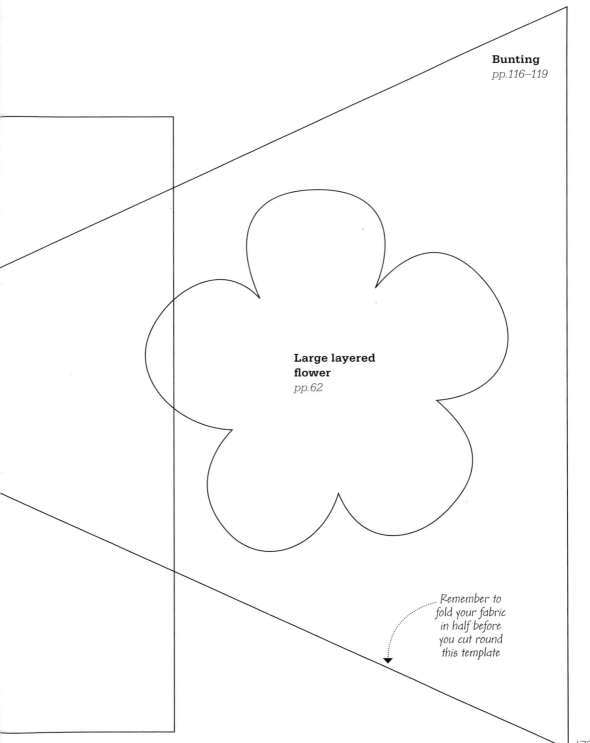

Bunting
pp.116–119

**Large layered
flower**
pp.62

*Remember to
fold your fabric
in half before
you cut round
this template*

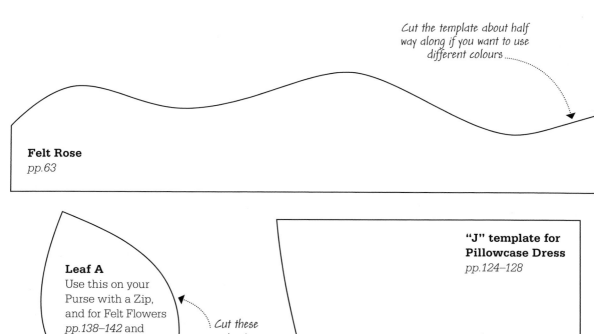

Cut the template about half
way along if you want to use
different colours ......

Felt Rose
pp.63

Leaf A
Use this on your
Purse with a Zip,
and for Felt Flowers
pp.138–142 and
pp.60–63

Cut these
out using
pinking shears ...

**"J" template for
Pillowcase Dress**
pp.124–128

Leaf B
Use this on
your Purse
with a Zip and
for Felt Flowers
pp.138–142
and *pp.60–63*

Leaf C
Use this with your
Felt Flower Brooches
pp.61–62

Bird wing
*Use this when making
your Alternative Bird
shape p.45*

180

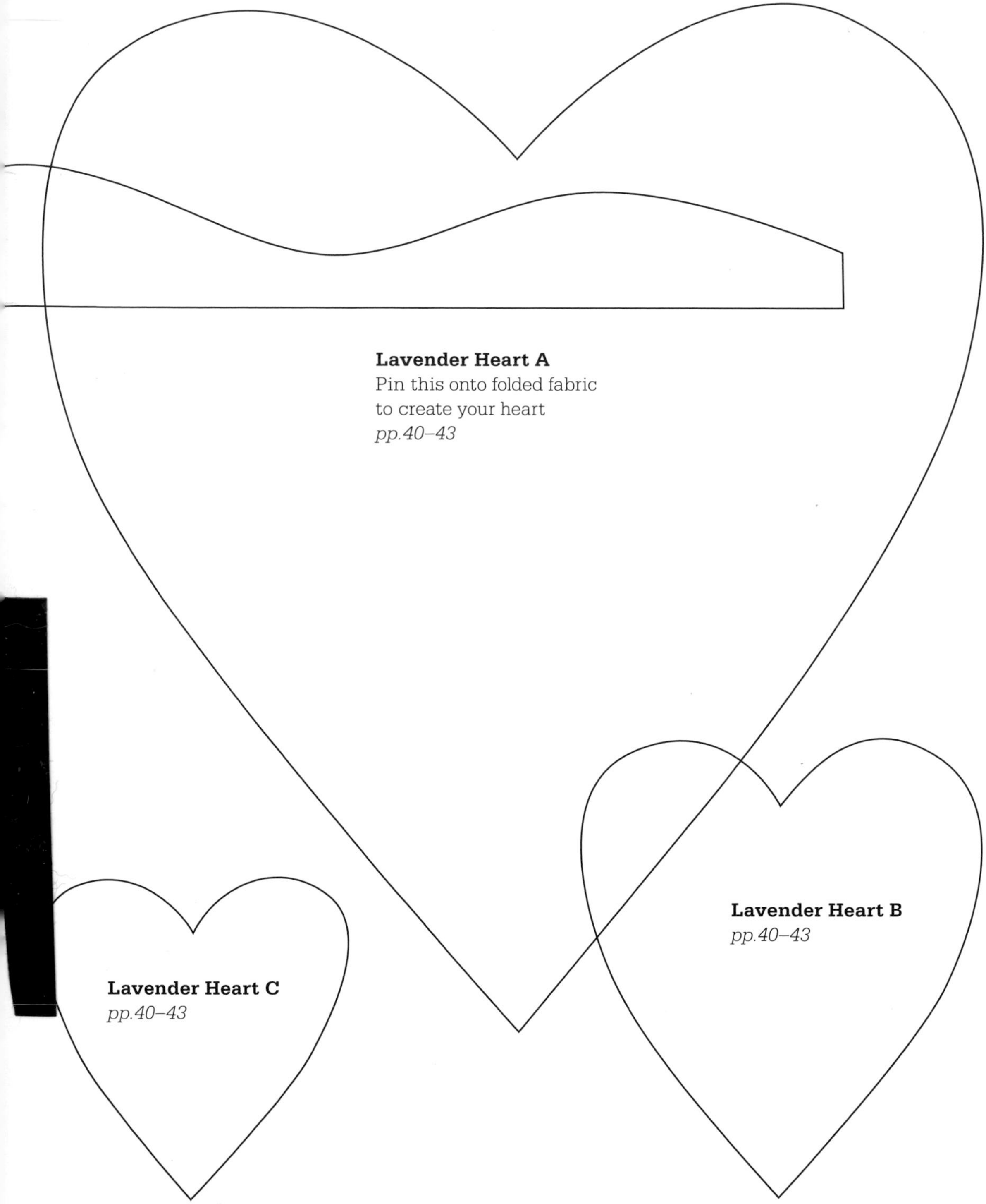

Lavender Heart A
Pin this onto folded fabric
to create your heart
pp.40–43

Lavender Heart C
pp.40–43

Lavender Heart B
pp.40–43

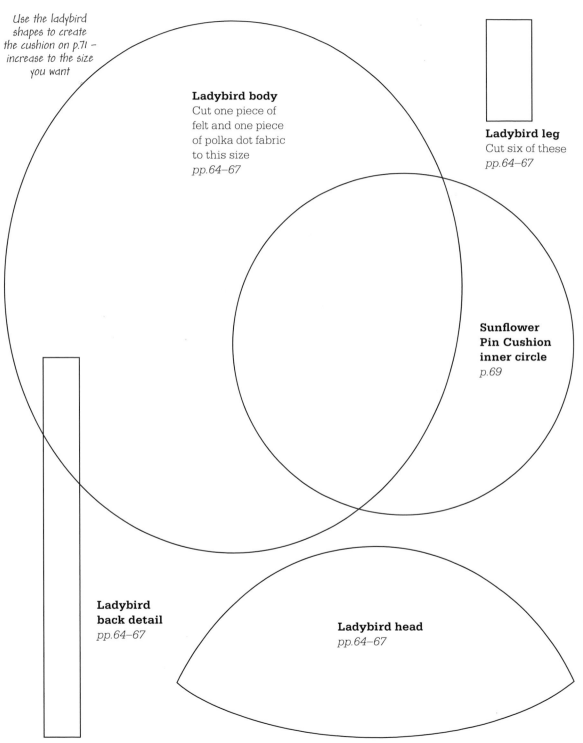

Use the ladybird shapes to create the cushion on p.71 – increase to the size you want

Ladybird body
Cut one piece of felt and one piece of polka dot fabric to this size
pp.64–67

Ladybird leg
Cut six of these
pp.64–67

**Sunflower
Pin Cushion
inner circle**
p.69

**Ladybird
back detail**
pp.64–67

Ladybird head
pp.64–67

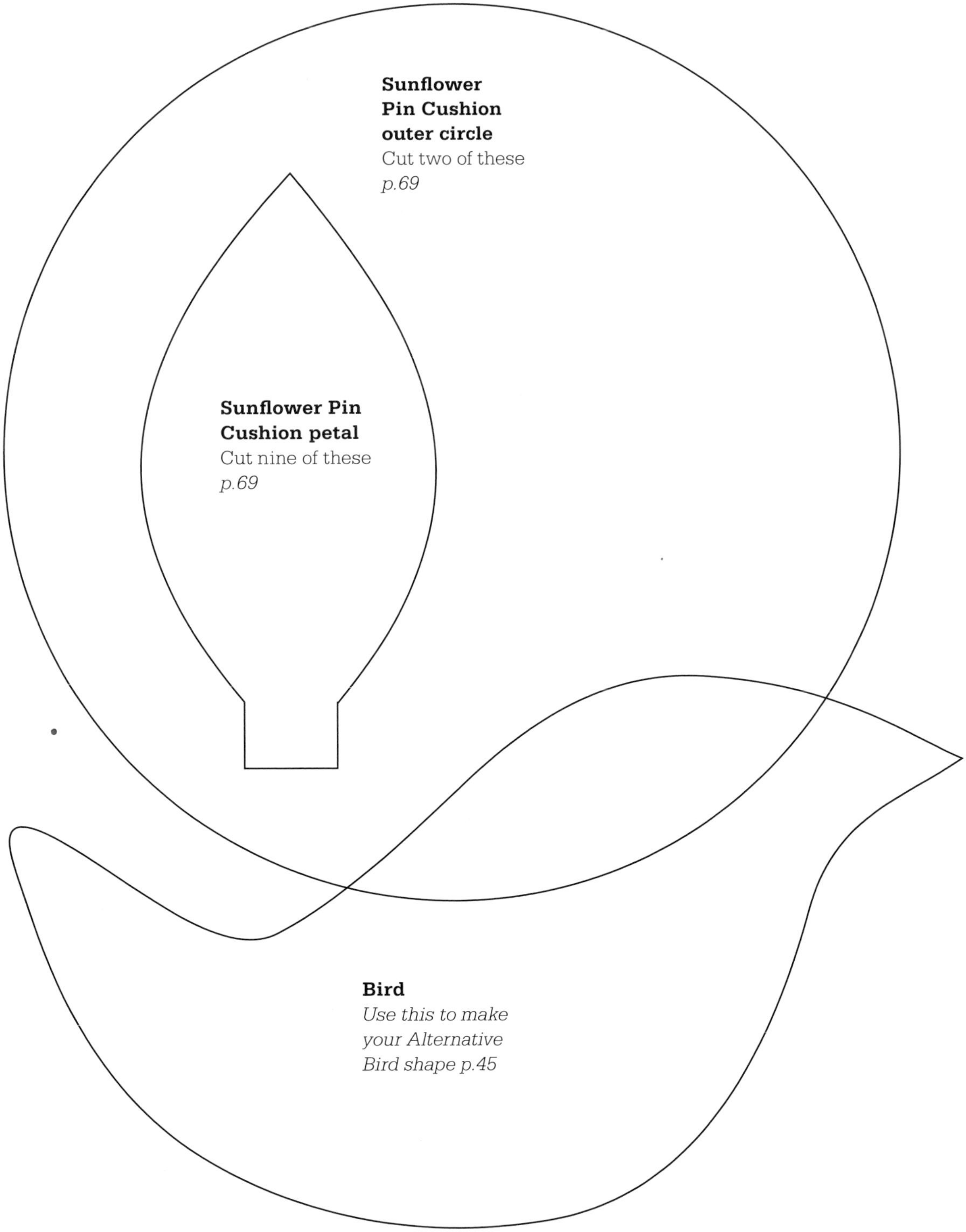

**Sunflower
Pin Cushion
outer circle**
Cut two of these
p.69

**Sunflower Pin
Cushion petal**
Cut nine of these
p.69

Bird
*Use this to make
your Alternative
Bird shape p.45*

Enlarging simple templates

The templates for these three projects are too large to be shown at full size.
The simplest way to create them is to use the dimensions given to carefully
measure them out and draw them up on tracing paper. They show the
correct positioning on the fabric and give the dimensions you will need.

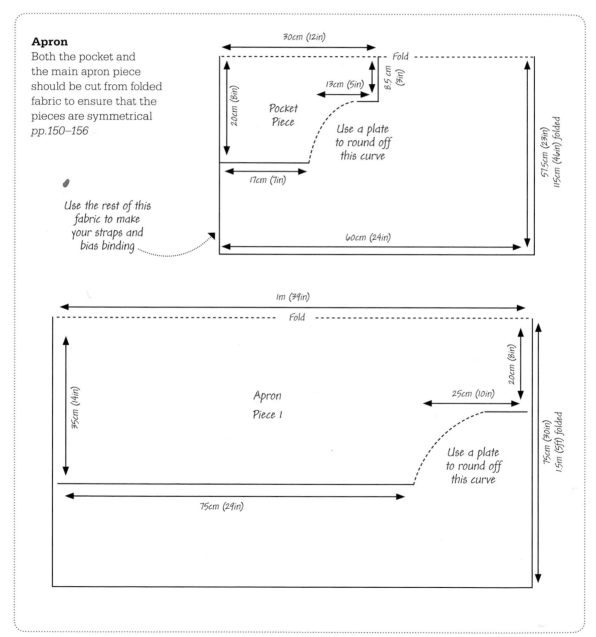

Apron

Both the pocket and
the main apron piece
should be cut from folded
fabric to ensure that the
pieces are symmetrical
pp.150–156

Use the rest of this
fabric to make
your straps and
bias binding

30cm (12in)

Fold

13cm (5in)

8.5 cm (3in)

20cm (8in)

Pocket
Piece

Use a plate
to round off
this curve

17cm (7in)

57.5cm (23in)
115cm (46in) folded

60cm (24in)

1m (39in)

Fold

Apron
Piece 1

35cm (14in)

25cm (10in)

20cm (8in)

Use a plate
to round off
this curve

75cm (30in)
1.5m (5ft) folded

75cm (29in)

Child's Shorts

Use your template to cut out two pieces of fabric, as each will form one leg
pp.172–173

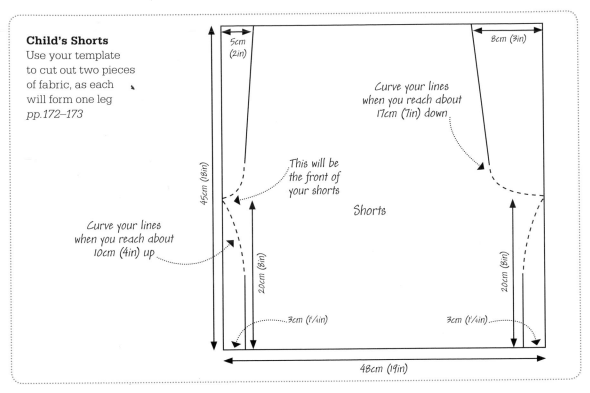

5cm (2in)

8cm (3in)

Curve your lines when you reach about 17cm (7in) down

This will be the front of your shorts

Curve your lines when you reach about 10cm (4in) up

Shorts

45cm (18in)

20cm (8in)

20cm (8in)

3cm (1¼in)

3cm (1¼in)

48cm (19in)

Door Hanging

Arrange your pieces like this to avoid wasting any fabric and to ensure that any patterns on the material align
pp.158–162

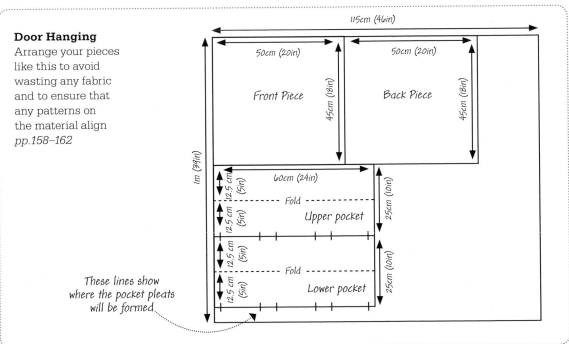

115cm (46in)

50cm (20in)

50cm (20in)

Front Piece

Back Piece

45cm (18in)

45cm (18in)

1m (39in)

60cm (24in)

12.5 cm (5in)

12.5 cm (5in)

Fold

Upper pocket

25cm (10in)

12.5 cm (5in)

12.5 cm (5in)

Fold

Lower pocket

25cm (10in)

12.5 cm (5in)

These lines show where the pocket pleats will be formed.

Index

Acknowledgements

Photographic Credits

Dorling Kindersley would like to thank **Dave King** and **Andy Crawford** for new photography.
pp.**22 Laura Knox** © Dorling Kindersley; **31** (top and bottom), **34–35** (all images), **36–37** (all images), **39** (all images), **56–57** (all images), **58–59** (all images): **Jane Bull** © Dorling Kindersley.
All other images © Dorling Kindersley.
For further information see www.dkimages.com

Publisher's Acknowledgements

Many people helped in the making of this book. Special thanks are due to **Caroline Bingham**, who designed and made up almost all the projects featured in this book, and to **Naomi Shackleton** for her upcycling projects on p.123.
Dorling Kindersley would also like to thank:

In the UK
Design assistance Jessica Bentall, Sunita Gahir, Vicky Read
Editorial assistance Martha Burley, Claire Cross, Kathryn Meeker
DK Images Claire Bowers, Freddie Marriage, Emma Shepherd, Romaine Werblow
Indexer Chris Bernstein

At Tall Tree Ltd
Editor Joe Fullman
Designer Jonathan Vipond

In India
Assistant Art Editor Karan Chaudhary
Art Editor Devan Das
Design assistance Ranjita Bhattacharji, Era Chawla, Anjan Dey, Prashant Kumar, Tanya Mehrotra, Ankita Mukherjee
Editorial assistance Kokila Manchanda

HARTLEPOOL BOROUGH
WITHDRAWN
LIBRARIES